Lead Change

Your Guide to Connecting Generations in the Workplace

Chris Cano

Copyright 2017 by JLH Publishing
JLHLEADERSHIP.com

Dedicated to my family:

Thank you Jessica, Lelia, and Henry for all of your unwavering support!

Table of Contents

Table of Contents

Introduction

CHAPTER 1

The Real Millennial Question

CHAPTER 2

The Generational Divide

CHAPTER 3

What Do We Know?

CHAPTER 4

Essence of a Pact

CHAPTER 5

Management vs. Leadership

CHAPTER 6

Who Should be Responsible?

CHAPTER 7

Personalize the Experience

CHAPTER 8

Autonomy is Non-Negotiable

CHAPTER 9

Communicate

CHAPTER 10

Teaching is the Future

CHAPTER 11

Practical Application of the Millennial PACT

Conclusion

About the Author

Notes

Introduction

I recently attended a conference and had the pleasure of speaking with many of our new and future leaders. These leaders are in their early to mid-twenties, and are referred to now by most people as Millennials. As I spoke to them, there was a reoccurring theme as we talked about how their acclimation to the work place was going. The vast majority felt that their education and experiences to date had not prepared them for the world they were stepping into. They had a desire to lead people, but had a hard time assimilating into organizations. That rough transition led to challenges with their peers and bosses, which ultimately led to issues with their teams.

This new generation of leaders and employees has been stereotyped heavily by employers, the media, and just about anyone else with an opinion that is noteworthy. The terms— "narcissistic", "disrespectful", and "entitled"— are frequently used to describe an entire generation of workers. The reality is that as employers, we could not be further from the truth. This generation is predominantly made up of educated, innovative, and motivated individuals that need guidance and direction to understand how to be successful in the organizations that we have built for them. Sure, their definition of longevity looks much different from that of their predecessors; additionally, their outlook on what it takes to be successful is also very different. As the mentors that have been charged to guide them, we must understand where they are coming from, what influences them, how they learn, where they find support, and what we can do to influence their growth.

If you are an employer and you are reading this, then I want to thank you for taking the first step in creating an environment that will not only attract Millennial talent, but will also foster retention. You are taking the first step in tearing down stereotypes, and will ultimately reap the benefits of having a passionate and engaged workforce. This book will provide you with information and systems to activate the benefits your team brings to the table, and capitalize on the potential that they exhibit.

If you are a Millennial and reading this, then you are going to be looking at this book from a couple of perspectives. First, you should look at some of the difficulties that your employer is having connecting with you, and creating an environment for you to thrive in. You need to understand that to make an impact in the future, you need to understand the past. The rules, processes, systems, and norms of the organization you are joining, or are a part of, are extremely important to the people that work there. The more respect you pay their accomplishments, the more support and empowerment they will give you. You will have plenty of accomplishments of your own someday, and I am sure you would appreciate the same from the incoming generation. Next, you need to answer most of the questions for yourself as you move through the book.

The more prepared you are to help your employer, the more symbiotic the growth will be. Understand that amenities, perks, and services are great, but their value is usually fleeting. Work to build the things that connect you to your company's mission, vision, and values so that you will be able to do the same for your future teams. Finally, if you lead people already, then you need to read this book from both perspectives, working as a Millennial and an employer.

Thank you for taking this step. Please feel free to reach out to me at any time at www.jlhleadership.com.

CHAPTER 1

The Real Millennial Question

The children now love luxury. They have bad manners, contempt for authority; they show disrespect for elders and love chatter in place of exercise. – Socrates

The tone of the room turns to one of silence and reflection as an executive volleys the thought that the reason turnover is so high, and productivity continues to suffer, is that this new generation of Millennial leaders does not have the same focus or dedication as their predecessors. Furthermore, our inability to manage them has led to greater concerns, though the concerns were never really addressed. The forty-five or so leaders in the room all nod their head in passive agreement.

This training class that we were all attending was one of the standard corporate classes designed to build leadership skill in one area or another. It focused on generating conversations that led to actions designed to improve the work life of the team, thus improving the performance of the organization. One of the standard exercises was splitting the room up into quarters and rotating through a SWOT analysis for the organization. Many things became similar trends across all of the groups, but one became particularly evident: that those in attendance were struggling to connect with the new generation of leaders, the Millennials.

Most in the room had opinions about the generation, but as we cursorily dipped our toe into the conversation, most were simply using buzz words that they had heard somewhere. The terms—"entitled", "selfish", "narcissistic"— were brought up but, in equal measure, the thought that they were extremely educated, innovative, and passionate was acknowledged. After just a few minutes of banter, a more prominent leader in the room basically stopped the conversation and asked the room to simply move on.

This conversation encouraged me to talk to some of my leaders when I returned to my property, to gauge their thoughts on the subject. Most of them are Millennials so their thoughts revolved primarily around being misunderstood. One of them brought up an interview that Simon Sinek did on the "Millennial Question" for Inside Quest. I had not seen the video, but I promised the team that I would watch it. Apparently, about five million other people had seen it to this point, which made me feel a little like I was hiding under a rock somewhere.

To be truthful, I had never paid much attention to the "Millennial Question". As a leader that was born in 1979, I was basically the tail end of Generation X, and just before the start of the Millennial Generation which is largely identified to start somewhere between 1980 and 1984. For me, these were my peers, and I had just simply been a little ahead of them. The generational question that I had struggled to answer during my career was how to lead older Generation X or Baby Boomer leaders as a relatively young leader. The thought of being worried about leading people younger than me had never crossed my mind.

As I watched the Simon Sinek video, I learned a few things. The first thing I learned is that the generational divide had apparently been given a name, and that it was ever widening. Sinek began to attribute the concerns of the Millennial Generation to four things: parenting, technology, patience, and environment. He cited a few studies throughout the course of the fifteen-plus minute analysis, and at the end, I was left with more questions than answers. I then proceeded to watch dozens of responses on YouTube, watched several TED talks discussing the generation, and began to read the research that most of these thought leaders cited.

As I returned to Sinek's video, two statements stuck with me. First, that Millennials are looking for ways to acculturate outside of their family into the greater tribe. I attended a talk where Seth Godin was the keynote speaker, and he touched on the thought of tribes. Godin's definition of a tribe during that talk was "a group of people that care about each other, their goals, and their culture". As this new generation of workers and leaders matriculate into society, they are struggling to find a means to connect to a group or organization because, in many cases, they can't identify the culture of the group they are joining. Sinek points out that the evolution of the corporate structure will start moving to one that attempts to connect passion and purpose to this new generation of leaders. Corporations are finding out that, as Godin points out, "you can't be a tribe of everyone". Defining what matters to the company, and synthesizing that into a connection with this new generation will start to form the tribe that they are seeking to acculturate into.

The second thought from Sinek's Millennial Question interview was that there is a "lack of good leadership". Godin further supports this by identifying that we "have a shortage of leaders that help us connect and grow". As organizations and corporations start to try and make a meaningful connection with a new generation of leaders, they are also struggling with a gap in good leadership that has permeated most levels of their entities. The 1980's and 1990's leader that was a title and a directive has fallen by the wayside and, in their place, is an expectation of a leader that is a coach or mentor and less of a boss. During the training class I attended, one of leaders said that they get frustrated because you can't just tell someone to do something anymore. That simple statement illustrates the much larger issue: that we have grown a society filled with managers, and very few leaders. Developing leaders that understand that building connections and growing their teams, leads to success, may be the answer to the Millennial Question that people are so intently asking.

Sinek explored several more controversial reasons for the widening gap between Millennials and the generations that preceded them, from the way they were raised, to the connection between social media and addictive behaviors seen in alcoholism and smoking, to the impact of technology on people's ability to connect. All of the thoughts were supported by research, and do begin to address some of the reasons why there is a perceived divide between the generations. Sinek never really provided his answer to the question. His postulated thoughts were intriguing and stimulating, and to his credit, in a later video, he asked for constructive feedback to help grow the thought leadership on this subject.

Maybe the real "Millennial Question" is less about the nuances attributed to this generation, and more about the way that we communicate as leaders. Just like with previous generations, the answer always lies in the evolution of our norms, and the way that we communicate those norms to our teams. There will always be things that earmark generations, but one consistency is that once you find a way to inspire and motivate them, the larger challenge lies in gaining their enrollment through communication, connection, and action. A further look at the last statement breaks the key components down into four words: enrollment, connection, communication, and action.

Enrollment

The summer months are particularly busy at the hotel I run, and as the General Manager I make it a point to be on the floor most of my day. One day, I went by our restaurant during lunch, and as they were busy working, I jumped in to help. After taking a few orders and clearing a few tables, I went to one of the senior servers, and asked him if we were missing someone. He replied that he had not seen Miguel for a while, and that the restaurant was backing up as a result. As I asked around, another server said he saw Miguel walk out towards the beach. I quickly headed that way to hopefully track down my missing server. When I arrived, I found Miguel staring at the ocean. I walked up next to him, and I suppressed my urge to aggressively ask him why he was out there. Instead, I simply asked if he was OK. Miguel looked at me and said that he didn't come all the way from Cuba to not matter, to just be a server at a restaurant. I asked him what he wanted. He told me that he wanted to make a difference in the lives of other people, but didn't think he could do that where he was. He said he joined our company because of the unlimited opportunities, and had been stuck for more than a year as a server instead.

Most leaders I have met would have stormed out to the beach and, because this had been an issue in the past with Miguel, they would have simply fired him. Instead, I looked at Miguel, and simply asked him what he was doing about it. He said that he had applied for other jobs, but had not gotten them. I again asked him what he was doing about it. After a few volleys back and forth, he basically decided that he had really done nothing at this point to get where he wanted to go. I told him that growth happens in small measured steps done daily, and that it didn't just happen overnight. I asked when last he read a book that he wasn't forced to read in school. He replied that he didn't think he had ever read a book that someone didn't force him to read. I told him that maybe he should make his own choice to read a book about the things that he would like to do. I told him that my door would be open if he chose to take that step. He smiled and ran back to the restaurant.

About three weeks later, he stopped by my office and asked if we could talk. I told him I would love to. He said that he had just finished reading How to Win Friends and Influence People, by Dale Carnegie. He asked if I had ever read it and, a little stunned, I simply nodded. He spent the next 15 minutes downloading in excited detail the contents of the book. In those 15 minutes, I could see his engagement. A light had been turned on for him, and as he turned to the last page in his book, he started to see more clearly where he could go and what he could do. In that one simple action, Miguel had become enrolled in his future, and in our business.

Seth Godin identified that "the key to enrollment is having the right people on the right bus". Miguel and I began to discuss what his seat on the bus looked like. It was clear that he did not want to be where he was, and so I told him that we had a position open at the Front Desk. It would be a step backwards in pay, but it would give him a chance to work on all of the things that he had just learned from Carnegie. Miguel took the job. Six months later, he was promoted to supervisor, and six months after that, he became a manager. When I asked him what that meant to him, he simply said the money was nice, but he was finally in a position to make difference.

Enrollment will be paramount as leaders attempt to answer the Millennial Question. Finding a way to ensure that the connection between the organization and the individual inspires them to want to succeed. That inspiration will drive them to achieve results. A leader that simply dictates terms to their team will engender a disconnect with demotivated individuals in the wrong seat on the wrong bus.

Connection

The thought of connection has changed greatly since I was a child. When I was growing up, a connection was made face to face, and because those connections were generally hard to come by, they meant something when they were made. Growing your connections required that you maintained your current connections, and then took the time to explore the people that your friends and relatives were connected to. In order to foster those connections, you would have to set aside time to meet, write letters, call them on the phone (that was attached to a wall), and sometimes just hang out even if you had something else you would rather be doing. Those connections built friendships that required a solid amount of time and effort to foster and maintain, and when you lost one of those connections, it hurt.

Today, connections are different. There are so many more options for meeting people. The world has become so small, technology has become so powerful and, as a result, connections are being made instantaneously. The internet, social media, cell phones, and the like have made identifying and interfacing with people all over the world as simple as logging on, and sharing a thought, sometimes with just a picture. I don't think that many people would argue that today's connections aren't as robust as they used to be, but at the same time it is where we have evolved to, so finding a way to incorporate the new paradigm of a connection into our workplace could help to answer some of the questions that have been posed.

As an organization or business, finding a way to incorporate the concepts of lasting connections, and instantaneous connections, will build a stronger network with your team and ensure that those connections become assets.

Communication

There are more avenues than ever to communicate with and the reality is that the delivery method is not the issue with communication. The President of the Unites States of America tweets. CEO's and department heads alike blog, and new companies are entering the market every day that give team members more of a voice than ever before. YouTube channels and Podcasts provide team members at all levels with verbatim thoughts from their leaders on almost any subject that they could ever care to ask about.

One of the largest reasons that communication is breaking down today is not a lack of delivery methods, but rather a lack of trust. I don't know how many times I have heard the sarcastic phrase: "well, if it says so on the

Internet, it must be true". Since most of the communication that is done today is done through the Internet in some form or fashion, the default premise is that most of what is communicated lacks the credibility of truth. When communication lacks the element of truth, you lose trust. People all over the world are failing to truly communicate because developing trust has become increasingly harder to do.

Companies have long provided their employees with mission statements, mottos, and values that hang on office walls and usually are not exemplified by even the officers of the company. As the new generation of leaders are entering the work force, and searching for the mission of the company, trust is being broken with each leader that does not connect with the mission, vision, and values of the company. No number of tweets, Facebook live videos, or blogs can re-instill that trust.

Action

I have been told that the largest gap is the gap between thinking and doing. One of the most common examples of this gap happens to most people I have met around the start of a new year. Millions of people step on a scale, and Immediately declare that this is the year that they will lose weight. The gyms and health food stores are packed for the next 14 to 30 days while people try and achieve their goal of weight loss. What quickly happens is that more than 80% of people break their New Year's resolutions by the end of the first month.

In most cases, those thirty days are spent planning the weight loss, finding the right clothes to wear to lose weight, and probing friends about their methodology, usually hoping for a new pill or procedure to make the fat melt off. In order to lose weight, you have to take Intentional and measured steps daily, focused on achieving your goal. Too many people focus on the outcome and not enough on the steps to get there. People who successfully lose weight are either highly motivated, or highly systematic.

This new generation has more distractions than ever, which has resulted in more excuses than ever as to why tasks can't get done in a timely manner. They are one Netflix binge away from having great thoughts accompanied by good intentions put into action. Leaders that want to inspire growth in this generation must guide the team in the concept of execution through intentional growth.

The Millennial Question is one that all organizations and corporations must ask themselves. This question however must not be how to work with a group of entitled, narcissistic, selfish people that still live with their parents. That base premise is flawed to the point that it discourages actual growth within an organization. The opening quote from Socrates may have been read as a reflection of people's current views of Millennials. Learning to connect with a new generation has been a challenge throughout time, this generation is no different. Technology has sped up the way that people communicate and consume information. As a result, leaders are having to learn new ways to communicate, grow, and inspire one of the most educated and innovative generations in history. Understanding what the actual Millennial Question is, finding ways to bridge the generational divide, and consistently executing on reimagined means of engagement will ensure the future success of any organization.

CHAPTER 2

The Generational Divide

"Few will have the greatness to bend history itself; but each of us can work to change a small portion of the events, and in the total; of all those acts will be written the history of this generation". - Robert Kennedy

On January 21st, 2017, an estimated 15,000 people took to the streets of Omaha, Nebraska to protest for women's rights. The turmoil after the 2016 Presidential election led to many similar demonstrations all around the country. Activists engaged in peaceful protest in a manner that echoed efforts of the past. Omaha is of particular importance to me because my aunt marched alongside those 15,000 people to voice her concerns, not only for her rights, but also the rights of her children and grandchildren. A woman that graduated in the 60's was once again marching right alongside today's new social activists.

This is the same voice of a student that graduated in 1965. Martin Luther King delivered his famous "I have a dream" speech in 1963 causing people to march against injustices and segregation. Two historically iconic figures, Martin Luther King and John F. Kennedy were assassinated leaving the country feeling uneasy. The Vietnam War had been raging since 1955 engulfing the youth of America with a growing unrest as to why we were still there. In 1962, Rachel Carson's book, Silent Spring, launched an environmental movement that led to a focus on pesticides like DDT, and the proliferation of industrial waste affecting the environment. This, of course, was all followed by the impeachment of President Nixon. Just like in the 60's and 70's, Americans are actively protesting racial injustice, human rights violations, necessity of ongoing military action, environmental degradation, and political ethical transgressions.

On January 21st, in Omaha, Nebraska, the generations found a way to cross the divide and stand united for something that they believed to be important to protect. While generations may be struggling to find common ground in the office place, they are finding ways to connect like never before on social issues, and philanthropic efforts. This common ground can provide a road map to crossing the divide, and creating bridges that foster lasting growth for all parties involved.

In the workplace today we primarily see Baby Boomers, Generation X, and Millennials or Generation Y. Today, the commonly accepted year ranges for a Baby Boomer are being born from 1946 – 1964. Generation X were born from 1965 – 1976. Generation Y or Millennials were born from 1977 – 1995.   In my research, I have seen most of these dates with plus or minus four years. If you are on the line of one of these generations, you probably exhibit characteristics of both or lean strongly one way based on the influences you experienced growing up.

In 2008, I became the Director of Operations for the non-gaming side of a casino. My job was pretty expansive covering more than 500 employees in about a dozen different departments. I was in my mid-twenties, and found myself for the first time having to rely on building relationships with leaders and employees that were in some cases 40 years older than I was. Previously, my roles had been mostly through the front of the house of luxury hotels, so nearly every employee or leader was within 10 years of me. I remember my first department head meeting, where I realized that I was the same age as more than half of my leader's youngest children. At that point, I wasn't as much worried about earning anyone's respect as I was simply trying to find something to talk about that didn't make me sound like I was asking my parents if they could clean up their laundry before my friends came over.

On my first day, we had our first leadership meeting that went as well as could be expected. People found out a little about me, and they left with assignments; there was some measure of alignment, but I left with a mountain of homework. My first order of business was to go speak with my Director of Housekeeping for the hotel. Sarah was a no-nonsense woman who had been a professional housekeeping leader for more than 40 years. I was in her office for about three minutes when I heard people gathering outside. It was time for the daily housekeeping meeting where everyone met to get their assignments, seek alignment, and get motivated for the day. These meetings are fairly commonplace in the industry, and are a prime stage for housekeeping leaders to shine. Generally speaking, if you haven't been in housekeeping, you fall flat on your face because you don't have a way to relate to the team that is staring back at you. If you don't captivate them within the first minute or two, you are sunk.

Sarah gave me a half smile and said, "Come on, let's go meet the team." She said good morning to the team, and they replied good morning in a thunderous roar. Sarah promptly said, "This is Chris, our new Director of Operations," and then took a step back. The hospitality industry is a pretty high turnover industry, so I had seen this same scenario play out on many occasions. The new Executive stands up in front of the team and reads off their list of accomplishments and credentials, says something cliché, and then walks out before the meeting is over, to a faked golf clap. I wasn't about to be one of those guys. When Sarah turned the meeting over to me, the first thing I did was say good morning in the four languages that I knew (that was about all I knew in three of those languages). Housekeeping is a very diverse workforce usually consisting of team members that speak English as a second language. The room erupted with good mornings in their native language. I saw smiles staring back at me. As I picked out a few replies in the crowd, I was able to make my way through, shake their hand, and ask where they were from. Someone would say Haiti, and everyone from Haiti would raise a noise. I did this a few times, and everyone in the room was smiling. I told them I was from a lot of places, but Ohio was where I told everyone I was from. I simply said I was excited to be part of the team, and I couldn't wait to meet everyone over the next few weeks. My credentials, accomplishments, and business acumen never came up. I got to shake just about everyone's hand when they left the room, and we got things started off on the right foot.

As Sarah and I returned to her office, she looked at me and said, "That was pretty good." She thought that I would try and prove myself with my title or job knowledge like my predecessors had, but instead she said I saw them as people, and not housekeepers. I started off the meeting by asking about her, and we began discussing things I wasn't going to find on her resume. I asked her what her biggest challenges were, and she went through a myriad of organizational and systemic issues that she was having trouble getting through. She asked about me, my wife, and my background. We discussed the fact that I had been a Director of Housekeeping before, and that led to conversations about solutions.

The reason that introduction and meeting was so successful was because I didn't look at the team as housekeepers, or employees. I didn't fit them into stereotypes, or worry about their age; I looked at them as people. There has been a lot of talk about the differences in generations, but at the end of the day, everyone wants to be treated as a person, not a position, title, or generation. I left the four-hour meeting with Sarah and headed to the lunch room. I hadn't really met anyone else at that point so, as I exited the lunch line, a housekeeper flagged me over, and asked if I wanted to join them. I sat down and was introduced to not only the housekeeping team, but also a few members of a few departments that I hadn't met with yet. We had some great conversations, and those relationships helped me introduce myself through several of the other areas that I oversaw. Again, focusing on people as individuals overcame any age, language, or cultural barrier that would normally have been an impasse to communication.

I recently read an Inc. article that that referenced a concept from the digital analyst, Brian Solis, called Generation "C". The "C" stands for the "Connected Consumer", and refers to "anyone who integrates technology into their daily routine, regardless of age." The article later goes on to point out that there are many definitions from many people for the letter "C" in Generation C, but the key component is connectivity. This generation is made up of people from every current generation class, despite the fact that it is most commonly connected to the Millennial Generation. This generation lives an algorithmic, curated lifestyle that is not dependent on traditional media, and values the opinions of their social media networks above the canned testimonials of the past.

I will admit that I have been severely behind on the social media movement. I have sat through countless presentations and demonstrations on uses and best practices, but had a hard time finding a need for it in my daily life. Once I started to use it, I was shocked that, without fail, the first like, comment, or share I would receive came from someone older than me. That person was usually my parents' age and when you looked at their profiles, they were posting, interacting, and updating at a pace that would put my college-aged sister to shame.

The Generation C concept is outstanding because it illustrates the possibilities of what can happen when labels are removed, and threads are used to connect people to each other. One adjective that could be used for the letter "C" could be commonality. This simple concept provides a road map for any employer that is racking their brain trying to find ways to connect with any generation. When I had to connect with the housekeeping department, I simply needed to find something that we both cared about. Some of the most amazing relationships are built on finding common ground and growing from there. Think of every couple that you have met that has stayed married 40, 50, or 60+ years. They never start by talking about their differences. They start by talking about the commonalities between them that helped to strengthen and grow their relationships.

As an employer, the idea of a "connected" generation should be a breath of fresh air. You don't have to have the amenities of the GooglePlex, or funky office spaces that resemble adult playgrounds, but rather you simply have to identify commonalities in your team, and build through them. In the work place, Generation C could stand for culture. A group of people of all ages connected by the norms, practices, and environment that breeds and grows connectivity.

When I started at my most recent hotel, there was a significant amount of change as the property was doubling in size. That type of expansion leads to rapid hiring, and usually a higher than normal turnover. The workforce in the local area wasn't great, so in the first year of operation we saw more than 100% turnover. There were dozens of contributing factors, but at the end of the day, the largest one was our inability to connect to each other as a team. Leaders in their twenties were trying to engage a team that was, in many cases, two or three times their age, and this led to a myriad of shortcomings on both sides.

I attended a conference, and Jon Gordon was the keynote speaker. He spoke to our room full of executives about his book, The Energy Bus, and how it can be used to improve everyone's life through the power of positivity. The book was a simple story with a simple concept, and I took some notes, but didn't really do anything with it right away. When I returned the following week to my site, I observed literally dozens of interactions where communication and lack of connectivity was a detriment to the team and the overall operation. I decided that we needed a better way to communicate, and we needed to have something that everyone could get behind, or in this case, on board with.

I decided to launch an Energy Bus initiative at my hotel. I took the book, and worked with a group of about 25 team members from all levels to develop a great presentation that I would personally deliver. The concept was well put together, and there was already buy-in from a solid number of team members from all levels. I delivered the message over the course of a week to every team member in a small group setting. We posted the Energy Bus Rules, and the entire property helped to create values that we would all adhere to. The attitude, engagement, and even vernacular of the property changed. People were "getting on the bus". There were no "energy vampires allowed", and everyone was saying that they were "too blessed to be stressed".

Over the course of the next two years, our turnover plummeted to less than 15%, our employee engagement numbers rose from 73% to 90%, and we won dozens of awards including the coveted Resort of the Year which recognized outstanding achievement in every phase of operation. The trick wasn't the 12-foot bus poster with everyone's face Velcroed to it, or the posters, or even the commitment by the leadership to remove anyone that was not "on the bus". Rather, the results came from having a common set of cultural norms that provided us all with our own unique means of communication. This culture enhanced the "why" of the property, which was to deliver unforgettable experiences that make vacation dreams come true.

My aunt wasn't seen by the crowd in Omaha as a Baby Boomer, rather she was seen as an activist. Everyone in that crowd regardless of age, race, sex, or sexual orientation found a commonality that united them to a common cause. In the work place, we don't need to find a trick, or a program to bridge and bind generations, but rather we simply need to remember to treat everyone like a person, and find ways to connect those people to a common cause.

In order to find that common cause, it is important to better understand the Millennial Generation so that we can begin to effectively create the inroads of commonality that will lead to future success in our personal and professional lives. The rest of this book will provide some information on the Millennial Generation, and will point out some key non-negotiable traits that have been identified through extensive research from leading agencies like PEW, Price Waterhouse Cooper, and several more. The result will be an introduction to the concept I have called "Creating A Millennial PACT". This will be a set of guidelines to help establish the culture, commonality, and connectivity that your organization, and you as a leader, are looking for.

CHAPTER 3

What Do We Know?

"From my very first day as an entrepreneur, I've felt the only business worth pursuing in business is to make people's lives better". - Richard Branson

Earlier, I mentioned a book by Jon Gordon called The Energy Bus. It is a great story of someone that is able to overcome their own negative view of the world by finding positivity through a series of collective connections that led to amazing things for everyone involved. In this book, the protagonist, George, is told about ten rules for the ride of his life. Whenever I started to explain these rules to my team during the rollout, I always became stuck on rule number eight, "love your passengers". I always got stuck because we really aren't supposed to discuss love in the workplace, and if we do, it is usually accompanied by corporate relationship agreements, or the awkward discussion about sexual harassment.

In this case, Gordon uses the phrase "love your passengers" as a way to encourage people to get to know the team they work with. This is always a tough concept to teach because generally in the work place, relationships stop at a cursory level, and if they extend to a deeper level, then there is usually a business motivation behind it. As we work to integrate new generations into the workforce, knowing what motivates them, and getting to know them personally will be the difference between harnessing their potential and wasting their talent.

At one of the hotels I worked for, there was a new cook hired into the kitchen team. He was quirky and quiet, and he really struggled to integrate with the kitchen team. He didn't process things the same way everyone else did, and since this was his first job as a cook, he didn't have the practical experience to fall back on. At one point, the kitchen team became so frustrated with him that they asked the leaders of the department to consider removing him from their area. The Food and Beverage Manager did not want to make that call because she felt the cook had not received a fair shot. Randomly that night, the Manager was on Amazon looking for a book to help her come up with the best way to deal with building non-traditional relationships like the ones she was dealing with in the kitchen. She made a mental error and typed in the name of the cook that everyone was having trouble with. To her surprise, listings in the book section came up with his name. It turned out that, even though this cook was only in his early twenties, he had already written four books, and had also been recognized for his accomplishments in the art community. The leader started reading some of the available text and was able to gain some insight into how the cook thought.

With her newfound knowledge, she worked up a plan to combine the information she gained with a style that she could introduce to the team to get the most out of the new cook. It turned out that if you engaged his creativity, and gave him a platform to express his thoughts, he came out of his quiet shell and contributed to the team. The concept of personalizing the work experience to gain higher levels of productivity from team members is a fairly common leadership concept, but common knowledge doesn't always equal common practice.

There are countless studies, articles, and blogs that discuss what we think we know about the Millennial Generation. The Internet is full of TED talks, editorials, and YouTube videos that provide insights into this new generation, and business and organization leaders continue to digest this information at a fairly high rate making experts out of even the most passive observer. With all of this knowledge, there should be countless strategies that employ empirical data to help businesses forecast and project the needs of their new workforce, so that their future can be secured with the understanding that their product, group, or service will be well taken care of down the road. Unfortunately, there may actually be too much information, so all of this has led to analysis paralysis. I want to point some of what I feel are the most important points about this generation so that we can start developing strategies for capitalizing on the unique attributes that make them great.

10 Things to Know

There are a lot of them - A recent article in the USA Today points out that as of 2017, Millennials have officially become the dominant generation in the workforce. In fact, by 2020 the work place is projected to be comprised of more than 50% Millennials, and by 2025 that number will balloon to more than 75%. That equates to roughly 81 million workers in the workplace by 2025.

Social Responsibility Matters – This new generation is looking to challenge the Baby Boomers as the most charitable generation. Currently 84% of Millennials surveyed will donate to charity during the course of the year. Further, more than 72% will donate their time to a charitable cause.

They Are Connected – More than 75% of Millennials have a social media profile, which isn't entirely surprising, but when you consider the breadth of potential socioeconomic barriers, it is impressive. Additionally, more than 80% sleep with their phone by their bed leading to a constant state of connectivity.

Not Business As Usual – As many as 66% of this generation have a strong desire to be entrepreneurs. The success of young captains of industry, and the limitless possibilities that our suddenly compact planet provide, have inspired this generation to live their passions as opposed to servicing someone else's.

Innovation Matters – The corporate structure and rules are a major deterrent to Millennials entering the business world. More than 63% of Millennials believe that management's attitude is a significant barrier to innovation, and 61% believe that operational structures and procedures stifle innovation as well.

The Autonomy of Groups – The Millennial workforce is clamoring for more autonomy, but that autonomy comes with a caveat different from previous generations. They like the empowerment, freedom, and flexibility that comes with autonomy, but more than 70% of respondents are more excited about a decision they make when their friends agree with their decision.

Homeward Bound – One of the more prolific stereotypes of the generation is that they "all still live at home". In actuality, there is an estimated 30% of the generation that still live at home, but to be fair, many are still in school. School loan debt has ballooned to crippling levels, and parents are more amiable to it now than ever before.

Changing Roles in the Workplace – There are some sizable shifts in how this generation views the workplace environment. Many Millennials prefer a job rotation verses a more time-consuming promotion as their personal time is much more of a premium. They also believe that work output is king, and that factors like hours worked in a day, and years with the company should not be deciding factors when discussing growth opportunities.

Interviewing You – This new generation is looking to be connected to a cause, and if they can connect a cause to your business, they are more likely to engage with you. They also believe that the number one most important factor in taking a job is the opportunity for personal growth and development. Only 21% of Millennials surveyed made an employment decision based on pay. Payroll has become a "Threshold Issue".

View of the Top - Bosses are no longer viewed as a title, but rather they are expected to be mentors and coaches. Those mentorship programs become deciding factors in retention. They have also clearly identified that the number one reason that they leave their jobs is because of their boss.

The first time I did a presentation with this information, I was in a room of about 25 people, none of whom could be confused with a Millennial. These were my peers in the hospitality industry, made up of mostly site General Managers and corporate regional leaders. They had a genuine interest in the findings, and were excited to hear what they could do to crack the code of this new generation. As I went through the presentation, everyone was highly engaged, and they provided a ton of feedback. I hate to say it, but I may have learned more during that presentation than they did. There were some very insightful observations that showed that most of the stereotypes and generalities that follow the Millennial Generation are not believed by as many people as the surveys would have you think. One of the participants had more years of experience in the industry than I had been alive, and it was interesting to hear him say that, "you just can't tell them to do something anymore. You have to explain the value in that thing getting done, and then work with them to get it done." The team agreed, and they went on to say that some form of that probably should have been done all along. Now it is no longer a best practice, but rather a common practice.

     Leaders that are able to take some of this information and adapt it to their teams will be the type of environments that promote growth, collaboration, and mentorship. Those environments will equip leaders with tools far beyond compensation to attract premium talent. Environments designed around growth will foster more sustained results in the coming years.

CHAPTER 4

Essence of a Pact

"Service to others is the rent you pay for your room here on Earth". – Muhammad Ali

As you start to look into what a pact is, you have to start with the definition. When you apply it to people, the definition of a pact is: a formal agreement between two people or groups made to help each other. This is important because, as we move forward, we will be doing just that— working on ways for two people or groups to find common ground, and help each other succeed. Like with any agreement, emotion is a contributing factor to success. Marketers will tell you that ads and products become transcendent when they connect with the passion of the target audience. In addition to passion, there has to be a sense of authenticity with the product or service and the people providing them. As the Millennials continue to search for connections and purpose within the work place, they will seek out employers that can tap into their passions, and provide a sense of authenticity.

About a decade ago, I found myself sitting in a conference room surrounded by a number of people that looked a little different than I did. They were covered in tattoos and piercings, their attire for a business event was pretty much like that of a Friday night, and it was hard focusing on what was more of a spectacle between the hair color and hair gel. Pumping through the room was some very trendy music, most of which I had never heard. The room was adorned with images of Johnny Cash, Kurt Cobain, AC / DC and some artists that I didn't even recognize. I was at the corporate orientation for Hard Rock International.

I had just left Ritz-Carlton, where ladies and gentlemen serve ladies and gentlemen, for an opportunity with a brand that I had really only known for t-shirts and cheeseburgers. My business attire consisted of a well pressed suit, conservative shirt, and cap toed shoes polished to a high shine. I thought maybe that I missed the memo on casual attire, and immediately I thought this was going to be a long week. My dress-down clothes included a sport coat not the same color as my slacks...yes, slacks. I thought I had captured the Hard Rock spirit by leaving my ties at home. I had two, but that's like nothing for a week-long business conference.

Just then a short man exploded on to the presenter's stage with a look more like Bono and an energy like Angus. Jim Knight had arrived. Jim was the cultural ambassador for Hard Rock International. He was charged with indoctrinating all new leaders with the Hard Rock Spirit. I was a bit thrown off, but at the same time couldn't help but get caught up in the excitement of the room. People in the room knew who he was, and looked at him in awe like he was a Rock Star.

My whole life had been a mixture of Mr. Marriott's staunch conservatism, and the exacting service culture of Ritz-Carlton. When I took my first leadership role as a management trainee in Washington D.C. at the J.W. Marriott, I remember having people come to me and ask if I was going to wear that olive colored suit again. I chuckled and asked why, and was basically told that if I wasn't wearing one of the same color suits as the photo of the two Mr. Marriott's hung behind the front desk, then I was going rogue.

Jim Knight quickly started talking about the Hard Rock culture, and I found myself enthralled by stories like how the first piece of memorabilia was collected when Eric Clapton wanted to reserve a seat for himself at the first Hard Rock Café in London, and did so by hanging his guitar over the seat. Pete Townsend, and then thousands of others then followed suit by donating memorabilia to what is now the largest collection of music memorabilia in the world. The unbridled spirit of the company that led them to destinations all over the world creating cafes that sometimes resembled more art than architecture. Their spirit to serve others that permeated every facet of every program that was rolled out by the company was intoxicating.

I became connected though with two words that Jim used, and the way that he talked about them. He said that the spirit of the company was authentic. That everything they did had to be authentic or guests wouldn't buy in to the culture. To further illustrate his point, he handed out the handbook which was a small burgundy book with a velvet cover. Yes, a velvet cover. Inside the book was the heart, soul, and spirit of the company. Jim proceeded to talk to us about how important it was that this book had heavier weight paper, that the type was a certain font, that it was organized in a certain way, and that the velvet cover helped to capture the irreverent spirit of the brand.

The word "irreverent" also stood out to me. I had heard the word used before, but never in a business setting. Most companies that I had dealt with would have shuttered if someone described their business or team as irreverent. Instead, the Hard Rock embraced an irreverent spirit that was forged by punk rockers, philanthropic pioneers, and tattooed servers alike. That spirit led to innovation and growth through a culture that embraced everyone for who they were, with a motto of Love All, Serve All.

As I heard the word 'irreverent', the thought of a runner from Coos Bay, Oregon, could not help but slip into my mind. I had really taken to running that year, and was literally reading everything I could find on the subject. In my reading, I came across the story of Steve Prefontaine. A runner from Oregon that changed the running world forever and was the inspiration for a mega brand. Pre became known for his brash irreverent style. He often spoke of his running as art, likening his time on the track to the efforts of a painter or composer. One of my favorite Pre quotes is, "a race is a work of art that people can look at and be affected in as many ways as they're capable of understanding". He was an authentic figure in the sport of running, and will always be remembered as such.

If you have ever run a race of any distance, you know that the most authentic moment of any race is the second you cross the finish line. Even the most seasoned runner cannot help but bear everything that he or she is during that one pure moment in time. The runners-up become equals as they are cloaked in the feeling of pride that accompanies even the most disappointing finish. Cheers and congratulations are the jubilant reward for everyone that crosses the line, and the awe and admiration of the spectators helps compose the song of your heroic deed.

Clad in compression spandex and wrestling with my bright pink swim cap, I couldn't help but let my ears drift to the groups of people that had gathered to join at the start line on this beach in Delray, Florida. Their conversations were filled with thoughts on their latest addition to their outlandishly expensive bikes, or discussion of their split times in the pool, or even the occasional proclamation of their finishing times which would be hard for any mere mortal to beat. The start line of my first sprint triathlon was very different from anywhere I had been before. I found that, if I asked the elder statesmen for advice or clarification on the course, they were very willing to indulge me and even engage in the occasional conversation about their first time. Having only really ever done running races, the triathlon was already starting to turn me off as I was having a very hard time connecting.

The race began and as we fought the swelling waves to get out past the brake, I found myself literally fighting off other swimmers as they tried to crawl over me to get an advantage. As we exited, I clumsily transitioned to my bike, and endured 10 miles of people yelling "on your left" as they flew past me. Nearly defeated, I dismounted and began to run. The distance was only a 5k, but in that short time I flew past more than 50 people. The runner in me kept saying things like "great job" or "you look great". I crossed the finish line and, to my surprise, was received with high fives from many of those people that seemed annoyed by my presence just about an hour earlier. I found the authentic spirit of the triathletes at that finish line, and it inspired me to keep going for a number of years in the sport. The competitive spirit drives all of them to achieve things most people couldn't dream of, and at the end, each of them can respect and admire the accomplishments of everyone that steps foot on the course.

I will always remember the Ritz-Carlton Credo as it is the heart and soul of that company, and I will always remember what it felt like to hold that little book while listening to a man speak with a singular passion for everything that was inside of it. Those two things to me are the essence of being "authentic". Businesses that know who they are and can convey that message to their teams instill a sense of authenticity and passion that inspires and engages everyone in the organization. That authenticity and passion are the answers to most of the questions or problems that anyone in that organization may face. When a leader possesses the same authenticity and passion, then people can't help but follow them. The one great authentic moment will engage and inspire those around you to follow you passionately.

Ask yourself these questions to help identify your authentic leadership style:

1. Can you think of a time when you, as a leader, were able to truly inspire those around you to action without the benefit of your title?
2. How would you describe your leadership style to a spouse, parent, or other loved one that knows the authentic you?
3. What actions do you take as a leader to enliven your authentic leadership style?

The authentic leader caries themselves in a manner that exudes confidence in their abilities, team, and organization. They possess a dogma that people gravitate towards, and can convey that in a manner that is educational and enlightening. This leader is not afraid to make mistakes, and support others that have failed because this leader knows that failure leads to growth.

Employment can now be seen as two sides coming together to pursue their passions to the benefit of each other. If these sides were to enter into a pact together, the base premise of authenticity would be non-negotiable. The same genuine, passionate spirit that fuels organizations like the Hard Rock and Ritz-Carlton will lead to differentiating factors that connect both sides to the future. Employers need to be prepared to find ways to tap into the passions of the incoming leaders to ensure that the same pure feeling I experience while racing can be found in some facet of the job. If this generation doesn't feel like they can make an impact in their roles or trust the leaders they work with, then they will continue on to an employer that can fulfill that need.

One characteristic that connects most hospitality organizations is their version of a spirit to serve. This is not just something that is spelled out as a process for the betterment of the guest, rather it is an ingrained dogma that drives us to help our communities. I have been part of the Marriott family for more than 30 years, and the spirit to serve is one of the strongest connections that I have to both the organization and my desire to help the people around me. It's philosophy that teaches us all to support and serve the community and organizations that support and serve us. During my time with Hard Rock, I learned to Love all and Serve All. Regardless of the organization, there is a connection that can be fostered and grown into a point of passion and authenticity with new employees, which in turn can activate their desire to make an impact. If your organization does not have this philosophy, then to start, you must do so through the passionate activists in the organization even if they are not in HR or are the CEO. Authentic passion will fuel your spirit to serve.

As we jump into actually creating a PACT, it will be important to remember that authenticity and passion are the fuel for building a bond between generations. As we learned earlier, the Millennial Generation is looking for a cause to connect with, and is willing to put in the time and effort to achieve an impact result. As employers, we need to make it clear from day one where their passion should be focused, and also to make the transparency of authenticity our currency.

CHAPTER 5

Management vs. Leadership

"Management is doing things right; leadership is doing the right thing". – Peter Drucker

Authenticity and Passion are now expected in the workplace, and they are the basis for new generations becoming inspired to put their best foot forward for whatever organization they function in or cause they choose to pursue. This generation has grown up in a business world that has preached the difference between a manager and leader, with the once vaunted manager coming up as a short-sighted task master when compared to their enlightened counterpart, the leader. This comparison is extremely important to examine before moving forward because every Millennial that enters the workforce is told that they need to be an ascended leader and avoid the drudgery of the manager.

This comparison is unfair, and is leading to many of the issues that Millennials are having in the workplace. The reality is that our current corporate environment and many organizations were built on the premise of the manager being the business unit leader. The definition of a manager is simply someone that is able to direct others to execute processes that produce a predictable result. Most corporations have a litany of processes and procedures, and they flaunt those processes as controls to ensure that a result will be achieved. These processes are usually easy enough to learn, but a manager is required to ensure they are followed. If those processes are not followed then the results that dictate the future success of an organization are not able to be produced consistently enough for others to develop trust. When trust is lost, then things like reputation suffer, and that leads to a decline in obvious monetary metrics like stock price.

Travelers and families alike have flocked to the Marriott brand for more than 80 years because of the consistently excellent experience that they deliver worldwide. People know that there will be cleanliness standards that are adhered to, that the Front Desk Agents will be friendly and knowledgeable, and that all of the modern comforts will be available. If you go behind the scenes, you will find binders and intranet sites dedicated to standards that can be translated into any environment that the flag is flying in.

As Millennial leaders enter this environment, they are asked to be something that they are told to run away from. They are told to be shepherds of the predictable. They are directed to learn and adhere to hundreds of standards that define every interaction, aspect of product, and even personal conduct. This expectation of consistency is what allows businesses to make decisions that lead to growth. This same model can be found in many organizations across dozens of industries. The industrialization of our culture was founded on our ability to be able to produce consistency from randomness. Unfortunately, the managers that have helped us achieve those results are being cast as the villain in the profile of a leader.

There are literally hundreds of definitions of a leader and most of them have to do with a few key words like "inspiration", "vision", and "achieve". A leader is someone that inspires others through their vision to achieve results they never thought possible. As new leaders are entering the workforce, they are being challenged to change the world, and to create businesses that are not only revolutionary but also socially conscious. The leader is someone that mentors and coaches their employees, and is an inspiration through their adherence to a vision.

When I graduated college, I was accepted as a Management Trainee for Marriott. I was stationed at a premier hotel that was a flagship of sorts for the company. The General Manager for the resort was a man named Charlie Perkins. Mr. Perkins was a leader. He had a presence on property that was felt by everyone that he came in contact with. His mix of professionalism and humor instilled respect and confidence in the team, and when he spoke, we all listened. He lived the mission and vision of our company, and helped all of us live it as well. The property standards were always evolving and that evolution led to better results within the Marriott system. He selected leaders that were empowered and driven to succeed.

As a new addition to the property, and really leadership as a whole, I looked up to Mr. Perkins. One thing you could tell about him, was that he understood that there was a process to success. He had a military background, and that could be seen in many of his even most basic interactions. I remember an interaction I had with him during my first week of work. I was in the lobby, and he walked by to introduce himself. He asked me to walk with him, and as we approached the shoe shine in the lobby, he asked me to sit down next to him. As we sat down, the cheery Brazilian shoe shine attendant greeted Mr. Perkins and got to work immediately on his shoes. I was a little shocked because, as I looked at his shoes, I couldn't see a spec of dirt or a single scuff on them. He began to talk to me about the property, and what they were trying to accomplish as a team. When his shoes were done, he asked for the attendant to do mine. I had never had a shoe shine before, and can tell you that she had her work cut out for her. When she was done, my shoes looked amazing. Better than the day I took them out of the box.

We both stood up, and Mr. Perkins paid for both of us. We both thanked the attendant, and continued on our walk. I should have known something was coming when the shoe shine attendant kind of smirked at me and shook her head as we walked away. As we finished our loop around the lobby, Mr. Perkins commented on how nice my shoes looked, and told me to keep them that way. As he walked away, I will admit that I was a little turned off. Of all the things he could have said to me, he felt like my shoes were the most important thing to discuss. I went back and talked to one of the Front Desk Managers, and explained the entire interaction. The manager chuckled, and began to tell me what the interaction meant.

He told me that everything had a process, and that process started with you. Each leader on site was the vision and definition of a standard that the property embodied. Our ability to care about the details leads to our desire to want to perform even the most menial task in the pursuit of excellence. Mr. Perkins expects you to adhere to standards and keep your team focused on their standards so that we can all move ahead. As he put it, imagine if everyone's shoes were shined, we wouldn't have to worry about that anymore, and we could all spend more time worrying about more important things.

This simple premise is why new leaders are having so much trouble adjusting to the environments they are entering. No one explains to them in school that if you can complete measured intentional tasks daily, you can achieve results that enable you to lead. Being a good manager is simply a cost of entry to being a great leader. Visionaries like Steve Jobs, Elon Musk, and the like, all understand that steps have to be taken to achieve their vision, and they need managers to make those things happen.

The discussion of a diminishing practice like a shoe shine may seem to be out of place in a book discussing the next generation, but it is at the heart of the divide between those leading in the working world today and those that are entering it. Mr. Perkins was able to make decisions about moving forward because he knew that he stood on solid ground. His team adhered to standards which provided a base level result that he could then elevate. His demeanor was consistent, and his thoughts were forward facing because he knew that he didn't have to worry about looking backwards, or checking his feet underneath him to make sure that his platform was still there for him to stand on.

The vast majority of new leaders need to understand the value of managing. There are very few new leaders that enter an organization and introduce such a visionary and inspiring performance that they reshape the business in a transcendent manner. In actuality, most new leaders are given a title, people that report to them, and are told to "lead" them. This reality suggests that the incoming leader knows the vision, mission, and values of the organization, and can then deliver a series of predictable results that would allow them to develop ideas that would inspire their teams to excellence. What usually happens is that leaders are given a title and a team, and within a few months, their leader is having to address a course correction because they have deviated too far from the company mission, vision, values, or norms. Their desire to breakaway and lead led them to jump out in front without observing that no one was following them.

In the 21 Irrefutable Laws of Leadership, John Maxwell discusses something called the Law of the Lid. This is a principle used to describe the leadership ceiling of a leader with the understanding that, if you can raise your lid, you can raise your performance. For example, if your leadership lid is a 6 then you are most likely performing at a 5. Maxwell says that it is entirely possible to raise your lid, and by doing so, you raise your potential. I explained this law to my team at one of the hotels that I ran, and after everyone had ascertained where their lid was, we had a great conversation about how to raise their lid. To my surprise, many of my younger leaders came to the conclusion that if they could start producing more consistent results daily, they could begin to raise their lid. They came to this conclusion because every time they talked about a barrier to performance, it usually started with an anomaly in their world. Despite having come to that conclusion on their own, they still shuttered when I told them that they just figured out that they needed to be better managers before they could be great leaders.

    The intent of this section isn't to tell future leaders that they need to learn to shuffle paperwork and be guardians of the latest standard operating procedure, but rather to save them some growing pains as they learn that management is simply a cost of admission for being a great leader. If they can understand the work that their teams do, and provide their teams with a beacon to home in on, then they can start to be the visionary leader that they were told they could be.

    As employers, we need to remember that Millennials are being told that they will change the world through their educated and innovative spirit. If we do not take the time to integrate them into the organization, then they will become frustrated with the box that we have built. Very few organizations have been successful at loosening the reins and bypassing years of process adherence to tap into this generation's true potential. Taking the time to merge the new vision of a leader with the real-world environment that awaits them will give companies and organizations the ability to invest in their future. If this understanding can be achieved, then both parties will benefit from the innovative spirit that is a hallmark of this generation.

Successful entrepreneurs understand that you have to be more than your vision. When you entrust your vision to someone else, there has to be a base standard that everyone operates at, or else vision gives way to chaos and frustration. Since more than 66% of this generation wants to be entrepreneurs, largely as a result of the existing crushing practices of our managers and confinement of processes, then it is imperative that we help them understand the place of management in their vision of the future.

If you are a Millennial reading this, then give your employer a break. Learn the history of your organization, invest in the processes that have produced the results that first attracted you to the organization, and don't come in with a disruptor mentality. You will find that the respect you pay your employer will be accorded back to you with the freedom and empowerment that you have been looking for. If you choose to simply come in and endeavor to "make an impact", then you will most likely become a statistic of the generation that quits their job because of their boss. Bosses aren't always great leaders, or in some cases competent managers, but if you learn the success factors of your company, it will entice people to invest in you. Almost every book on leadership will tell you to lead by example. If you show your team that you value what they have built, they will show you the respect and support you need to become the leader that you intend to be.

CHAPTER 6

Who Should be Responsible?

"You must take personal responsibility. You cannot change the circumstances, the seasons, or the wind, but you can change yourself. This is something you have charge of." – Jim Rohn

Right now, most of the literature and experts agree that companies and organizations should take the responsibility of creating environments where Millennials can thrive. Practices like flexible work hours, frequent and consistent performance reviews, and new boundaries of empowerment are designed to not only foster innovation, but also engagement. Employers are being encouraged to abandon old work habits and incentives, and replace them with new more trendy offerings and standards that will appeal to the next generation.

In many cases, this is a massive departure from the cultural norms of the organization. This shift may seem great for the leaders coming in, but in many cases, this is uncomfortable not only for the existing team members, but also the existing leaders. Many of these practices are great, and really do enhance the work environment for everyone, but it does, in some cases, lead to resentment at many levels. Existing team members and leaders will frequently allude to new members not "paying their dues", or being allowed to get away with things that were not previously allowed.

This resentment is nothing new. As long as I can remember, established generations are always looking at newer generations as having it easier. People are working less hours, they are getting more perks, benefits packages are more robust, and salary is much more competitive. In many cases, these perceptions may be true, but the reality is that this is how the work environment has evolved regardless of the incoming generation. People are working less hours because values are changing throughout our country. Millennials did not invent work-life balance, they are simply a by-product of the overcompensation arising from the generation that thought an 80-hour work week was a badge of honor.

The hospitality industry used to be a highly transient environment, people transferred to new locations throughout the world every 12-18 months. This was how you got ahead in the industry. You worked a ridiculous number of hours, were always available, and moved on command. With those moves came promotions, recognition, and increased compensation packages. Unfortunately, in many cases, it led to parents living in different cities, kids changing schools frequently, or simply a high level of burnout with a low rate of retention. To this day, I still have older guests ask me when my company will be moving me to the next site, because they remember when that was the norm.

As recently as the 2000's, I was one of those leaders. The expectation was that your value was attached to the number of hours you work, and that if you only worked 50 hours a week then you weren't a team player. In multiple organizations, I would work 14-16 hour days, and in many cases six or seven days a week. I was a leader in my twenties and was engrained with that mentality of work-life balance.   Basically, there is no balance— there is work, and then the occasional things you get to do outside of that paradigm. I would like to say that this was reserved specifically for hospitality members, but the reality is that I had many friends, family, and acquaintances that were held to the same standard in a variety of industries.

      The world is changing rapidly, and with it, people's definition of work-life balance. Millennials are being credited with forcing the shift, but nearly everyone I talk to now, regardless of their generation, has started to realize the value of the shift. The massive leaps in efficiency, seen by the connectivity that now exists, has opened the door for this new work-life balance to be achieved. Employees and leaders at every level are finding new efficiencies every day, and their employers are rewarding them with greater flexibility to pursue the things that are important to them.

      The hospitality industry is having to learn to adapt to this shift and, in doing so, has created programs that speak to the essence of this new generation. In many cases, leaders and team members are staying put longer in one location which is actually causing more of a log jam in the hiring and promotion process. As a result, new programs are being developed and highlighted that allow associates at all levels the opportunity to learn new skills. In previous models, you physically had to switch jobs to learn new skills. Now the best leaders are realizing that you can provide cross training and development which sets you up for future success. Instead of hoping that someone from another location applies for an opening that you may have, you are building a series of people that are qualified to move into those roles. This homegrown system is strengthening the perception that work-life balance is just as important as any other priority in the industry.

This same premise could be applied in nearly any organization. From a purely monetary standpoint, saving the money that would be used for recruiting and relocation will cover a good deal of the costs associated with cross-training. In this model, a two-way relationship is formed. The employer is providing the opportunity, and the employee is given the responsibility of succeeding on their own merits.

Moving forward this book will examine solutions in a symbiotic manner. There will be give-and-take between both employer and employee, and both sides will be responsible for bringing the PACT to life. The steps of the PACT are going to be written from the perspective of the employer as they are the ones that have to adopt the principles in the work environment for these programs to be effective. Once these principles have been implemented, the Millennial leaders will have a responsibility to be active in the participation of, and execution in these areas. We will learn to personalize the experience, create autonomy in the workplace, improve communication, and place a greater emphasis on teaching.

CHAPTER 7

Personalize the Experience

*"Conformity is the jailer of freedom, and
the enemy of growth". – John F. Kennedy*

There are many buzz words and phrases used in business to try and impart a sense of autonomy to leaders with the hope that they will take their organization to the next level. Words like "empowerment" and "leader", are brandished with little regard for the implication and intent of their use, and inevitably you are told to run the business as if it were your own. That sentiment feels great when your boss tells you that, but the application tends to be a bit more difficult.

I was 24 years old when I first told a direct report to run the department and team like it was their own business. It made sense, after all, my boss had said that to me and it had fired me up enough to get me going in the right direction. I told Darin to live our mission, that he was empowered to make the guest happy, and that he needed to make sure to take care of his team. I urged him to be creative, and think outside of the box to come up with world-class solutions. I am pretty sure that covers most of the clichés that are out there for giving direction for the first time to another leader.

Once I had Darin aligned with the rhetoric, I let him go. I let him go for about a day before I gave him his first corporate standard operating procedures manual. I followed that up by having him adhere to the local standard operating procedures, and wrapped that up by peppering him with memos of understanding that further defined his roles and expectations. Once the paperwork was turned over, I made sure he attended our corporate training classes, and completed his exhaustive e-learning requirements as well. At the end of all of that, I had painted a very thorough and complete box for him to live in, that would ensure that he was a proper manager for our company.

As I reflect on my direction to Darin, what I effectively did was tell him to treat the business like it was his own, but only if he adhered to a process, policy, or memo that I provided him. Corporations are great at doing this. We identify a set of norms that define success, and we try and produce as many people that fit those norms as possible with the understanding that those "teams" will have the greatest possibility of success. The growing issue with this mentality is that it is putting a generation in a box, and they are screaming to be let out. The process of doing this is exhaustive for managers, and is unproductive for Millennials. In my experience, I find that teams that learn "less is more" when it comes to policies, enjoy an evolving workplace with a lower turnover.

As we look to engage new employees and leaders, we need to determine the best way to create a more personalized experience that allows for growth, development, engagement, and advancement on multiple timetables, and not just standard progression charts. This sterile suggestion doesn't at all capture the emotion that is associated with all of these topics. Any one of these areas can elicit a passionate response that either energizes or deflates one of your team members. In many cases, things like engagement, development, growth, and advancement have been rallying cries for change in many organizations across the world.

Where most of us fail as leaders, is that we provide the tools for our teams to manage, and then we don't ever explain the "procedure box" is simply a platform to stand on to be great. The drowning conformity of managing through process will strangle this new generation. If employers want to make an impact, then the processes and procedures that I saddled Darin with have to be accompanied by an expectation and plan to connect them with the larger purpose, and inspire them to innovate and grow past the established standard of excellence. For this to happen, then leadership development must evolve into a combination of process and personalization.

The first step in creating a Millennial PACT is to "Personalize the Experience". From an employer perspective, this is going to be difficult because we have worked hard to create systems and processes that lead to predictable results, and those paradigms generally thrust people into the boxes I mentioned earlier. Personalizing the experience requires a far deeper commitment as it intimates that each individual in your organization is deserving of your time or the time of the leaders that report to you. Not only are they going to receive your time, but they are going to receive your efforts, and they are going to benefit from the marriage of the two. In kind, employees will be required to participate in order to reap the full benefits of the opportunities provided to them.

      A couple of key pieces of information from earlier provides a window into a direction to take personalization. Millennials choose a job based on their perception of the opportunity for personal growth and development. In addition, more than 66% of Millennials want to be entrepreneurs. These facts describe a group that is looking to grow, and looking to do so at their own pace. As such, employers need to take an active role in providing the tools, opportunities, and feedback sessions necessary for the new leaders to succeed. This personalization will require an understanding of the individual's personal desires and goals for advancement, and an understanding of how to navigate them through your offerings to help them arrive at their destination.

      In some cases, you may determine that your programs aren't sufficient to service the growth and development goals of your team. It will become incumbent on the leader to be open and forward thinking enough to involve their Millennial counterparts in the creating and implementation of new programs that meet the evolving needs of the workforce. By involving your team in the generation of new programs, you will gain buy-in, and will guarantee a higher level of participation and retention. In many cases, your world is evolving faster than you can handle, and creating these relationships and working paradigms will ensure you are competitive in your approach.

The following are examples of programs that you can implement to help personalize the employee experience:

Development Plan

The development plan is nothing new, but executing a successful development plan is something that generally escapes most leaders. In my experience, a development plan is a stagnant set of tasks designed to attain a fixed goal. That definition better fits an action plan that a manager can use to guarantee the successful attainment of a task, or conversely can be used to reprimand an individual for not completing that same task.

A development plan, on the other hand, is a fluid document designed to capitalize on the strengths of an individual created to help attain a desired state. A successful development plan will be a living document that changes as both parties grow. The practical execution of this plan requires a form that can be tracked and monitored, but the focus should be on information that will help your team member develop professionally or personally, should you choose.

The most demanding aspect of a development plan is the time required to execute it. The form should not be the focal point, but rather the follow-up, follow-through, and results produced should be the measuring stick of success for all parties involved. Interactions in general are being sped up, and the traditional review process of drudging through a form for an hour-plus is losing its place in the business world. A development plan session could be accomplished in as short a period as a few minutes. Both parties are well informed of the agreed upon criteria, they are both ready to follow up on commitments made, and they are both ready with next steps. The document is updated, and then they agree upon a next meeting time. I have even had successful development plan updates walking across the campus. If both parties are engaged, the process becomes much smoother. I find that the longer sessions are usually brainstorming sessions—those times when both parties decide that they need to execute a course correction, and then make the corresponding commitments.

Activate Their Strengths

Too often, people guess their strengths, or worse— your boss does. There are a number of existing tools that help to identify a person's strengths. Assessments like the ones provided by Meyers Briggs or other options, like the DISC Assessment or Strength Finders, provide outstanding information on a person's strengths. Knowing your strengths is paramount when determining what your growth will look like.

If you want to invest in your future leaders, then make sure they have taken a strength assessment, and that they know what those strengths mean. They will be much more productive and engaged if you can work together to find programs and assignments that allow them to activate those strengths. A strength approach to leadership is the ultimate personalized experience that ensures engagement.

Systems of Recognition and Reward

Just like everything else we have discussed, recognition and rewards are not one-size-fits-all. The traditional plans for recognizing top performers like "employee of the month" are becoming obsolete. Just like a development plan, Millennials want recognition and reward to be specific and commensurate with their accomplishment. As a result, employers are having to develop non-traditional systems to ensure they reach their target market.

Rewards like paid days off, schedule preferences, additional job opportunities, new benefits, and educational experiences are becoming the norm. Cash isn't as important as it used to be as we learned salary is more of a threshold issue than an actual deciding factor on engagement. The more specific that the team member finds the reward to be, the more value will be placed on it. Personalized recognition can lead to instant engagement regardless of the generation.

While it will traditionally be the employer that has to set up these systems and processes, it will be the employee that has to participate in order to reap the benefits. A development plan without active participation is simply an exercise in paperwork. The Millennial generation has to understand that personal responsibility cannot be given by their work, but rather has to be shown by them.

If you are a Millennial and are reading this then understand that if these opportunities are presented to you, then you must be actively engaged in their execution for them to be successful. You need to know what you want, and have an idea of what direction you would like to travel in. If you wait for someone to dictate where you are going, you will most likely not like where you arrive. It's OK if you start a job, and do not know even what the next step is, but it is incumbent on you to ask the questions and begin to form your own opinions. Be present, be active, and be engaged to reap the most out of the work that your employer is putting in. If you lead others, remember that you also have to go down this road with them.

CHAPTER 8

Autonomy is Non-Negotiable

"Synergy is what happens when one plus one equals ten, or a hundred, or even a thousand! It's the profound result when two or more human beings determine to go beyond their preconceived ideas to meet a great challenge". – Stephen Covey

The autonomy of teams is a growing trend that will be a hallmark of the Millennial Generation. As we learned earlier, they feel more confident about a decision when their friends or co-workers agree with them. Many employers now believe that Millennials want to be empowered to operate in their one-person army and accomplish their task at their own pace. The research starts to point to a much more social trend whereby small groups are more attractive because the support that is found in numbers creates a confidence that is desired.

As employers look to set up business models to accomplish their goals, they have to keep in mind that the concept of accountability has not been particularly reinforced with this new generation. The phrase "participation trophy" has been used on a number of occasions to describe how parents and educators have dealt with the Millennials. The idea that if you show up, you will be rewarded, is a dangerous trend. As that trend progresses to the work place, the participation trophy mentality leads to lack of accountability in many cases.

Employers work on deadlines with a desired level of achievement, and when that does not happen, the result is not a participation trophy, rather you are usually documented or possibly even fired. New leaders and entrants into the workforce will claim that they were not given participation trophies, and that their employer simply didn't set the right expectation of success. This argument could continue forever, except that, at the end of the day, the employer will be the one making the decision about your future employment. A new methodology for setting expectations and establishing accountability needs to be established.

When I was young, I played in one of those elementary school soccer leagues where everyone was required to play, and everyone got ice cream or pizza at the end. I was never particularly athletic so I ended up being the goalie for most of the season. At that age, the goalie isn't the agile monster cat lurking as the last line of defense for a team. Instead it is usually the kid who can't run, follow directions, or pretty much was a liability everywhere else except standing in a box. That was me. I was told over and over again that I was part of the team, and that I was good at what I did. The reality is that I was horrible, and the only balls I ever stopped were usually with my face. If you have glasses on, that can be particularly painful.

I would have loved for someone to tell me that I wasn't that good. Instead, I spent practice either being barraged with balls, running laps, or practicing kicking down field, which was my one responsibility. My poor mother had to buy about half a dozen pairs of glasses before we realized that soccer was not my sport. I still have plenty of trophies from those years, but had someone found a better way to motivate me or do something with me, I might not have been so beat up.

Finding a new way to align teams is easier said than done. Each industry and each job presents barriers at many different levels but, as we have learned, if you don't evolve, you die. More particularly, if you don't find a new way to engage these new leaders, and provide them a template to engage their leaders, then you are setting them up for successive patterns of failure.

If you look at the structure of social media, you will see that, while most profiles are individual, they rely on the approval of others to drive content, frequency, and engagement. Groups are established in many ways to join like-minded individuals to a cause, and immediately, you are connected to people that will provide you with feedback regularly. In a work environment, you are usually given assignments or goals, and your feedback comes from your boss. As employers, we need to figure out how to not make work a solely individual effort but instead, create connections to help provide feedback, establish systems of accountability, and foster an environment of positive growth.

Ideally, employers would be able to establish small groups or committees with a goal of solving a problem, or generating innovation within their space.

With our understanding of how this generation operates, the group would provide them with many of the latent needs that are not found in their current jobs. Small groups would offer differing viewpoints, would encourage social support, and would give the validation that is needed to feel confident with their approach.

During a speaking engagement on Millennial Leadership, one of the attendees made a very relevant observation about the differences in the generations. He said that he couldn't ever remember teaching his parents anything, but now things are totally different. He made a remark that, at a family dinner, he was having an issue with his cell phone, and his twelve-year-old nephew fixed it for him and even downloaded the new software. He realized at that point, that there is a symbiotic relationship between generations that could either be viewed as constructive or destructive. He went on to say how much he values Millennials in group work exercises because they bring a unique and savvy perspective to the table. At the same time, he also felt a responsibility to guide them and provide what knowledge he could, without trying to impress his decision-making paradigm on them.

The point of the story, as it relates to autonomy, is that the changing dynamics in the workforce need to be recognized, and if employers are able to build groups containing multiple generations, they can not only leverage their collective intelligence, but also create synergies and build relationships. A group would ideally be made up of 3-7 individuals with complementary skills.

I realize that this is not always possible, and when it is not, then the group should, at least, include different points of view to ensure multiple ideas and solutions are brought to the table. These groups should feature specific assignments with enough direction to make them functional, but also with enough latitude to allow them to succeed or fail on their own.

      Failure is a tough concept for many leaders to deal with. In most cases, failure is viewed as negative with the resulting outcome being grounds for disciplinary action. In actuality, failure in many cases leads to future success. Much like a scientist experimenting, your teams will do the same, often times resulting in less than sterling achievements. At that point, it is the responsibility of the boss to not get angry, but rather to work through the failure with the intent of getting to a future success. Failing forward is a concept that many leadership authors have touched on, but is still not widely accepted in the work place. Rather, too many leaders jump in before an employee or team fails, in an effort to effect a different outcome. By doing so, the leader has stunted the growth of the individual or team, and most likely still did not achieve a desired result. By supporting the group, and actually allowing them to create change, either positively or negatively, you are building trust. If that trust is not present then, the group scenario will simply be an exercise in futility because they will soon learn that they do not have the trust and support needed to make an impact.

When constructing a group think environment, leaders need to be ready to harness failure to accomplish their goals. The Millennial generation is not too familiar with failure so there is a risk of this being devastating to them. If they are put into small groups to accomplish a task, then the validation of the group will provide the autonomy they need to make decisions and push forward, regardless of the resulting conditions. Turning failure into victory is a key component of group execution.

At one of the hotels I worked in, we conducted time and motion studies to determine a way to make Housekeepers more efficient while cleaning guest rooms. We found that, in our business model, it was more efficient to pair Housekeepers into teams of two. The first couple of weeks we experienced ups and downs. Some teams performed outstandingly while others lagged behind. We saw some team members that really loved the changes, and others that were furious. As we started investigating, we started tracking the different productivity levels of different pairs. We thought that if we paired them with people they liked or shared themes of commonality with, then they would be more productive. Over the next several weeks, we worked on finding out each team's preferred pairing with 4 alternatives, in the event that someone is not there for the day. As we started to pair these teams together, we found that increases in the quality of relationships led to more productivity. Furthermore, if we paired those teams with inspectors they trusted, then the productivity continued to increase.

Leaders that are in tune with their teams are able to judge the various attributes of each player, and put them in an environment where they are supported and validated by the members of their group. When this happens, productivity increases, engagement increases, and innovation is fostered. Additionally, the paradigm governing the terms of failure are shifted. Group members are able to support each other with candid feedback, much like what occurs on social media. Affirmations are free flowing, and comments dictate the future growth, development, and execution of the group.

To further examine this phenomenon, I think the tribe mentality that occurs in many fitness groups is a great example of like-minded individuals coming together to support each other to reach a common goal. Over the past several years, a fitness craze has led to almost cult-like group followings all over the world. The CrossFit craze has led to tribes all over the planet that have developed into small group support systems to accomplish the goal of unreal physical fitness. The garage-style gyms have evolved into brick and mortar businesses that house fitness fanatics bent on pushing themselves to the absolute peak of physical endurance. Industries have evolved from their passion, comradery, and dedication to their craft. The tribe mentality can be seen in these groups, and can further be used as a model for creating effective groups in the work place. Lofty goals are clearly set and defined by the workout of the day format. Instructors and tribe members alike, motivate you to achieve things you never thought possible. When you fail— because you always do at some point— then the tribe is there to lift you up.

Another outstanding example of this can be seen in something called the November Project. Runner's World Magazine did a feature on a group called the November Project. This movement was started in Boston by Brogan Graham and Bojan Mandaric, Northwestern Crew Alumni, as a way to keep working out during the cold winters. This group now has chapters in 41 cities with hundreds of members all attending free-to-the-public workout sessions held in featured locations. These groups employ the tribe mentality, and just like the CrossFit members, they provide guidance, support, praise, and an antidote to failure.

These examples provide great blueprints of how small groups can thrive in organizations, and how, when combined with passion, this can ignite movement level growth. As employers look to connect with their leaders, they need to remember that, unless there are systems of support for new leaders, they run the risk of failure without progression. Like any initiative, if this is not fully supported at every level, then it will simply become something that has to be done, versus something that is a benefit to all parties involved.

If you are a Millennial and you are reading this, then help your leaders understand the value of groups. When you are given an opportunity to perform as a contributor to a group, take the responsibility seriously with the understanding that the more you invest in this process, the higher the likelihood that this will become a viable model within your organization. Groups are able to hold each member accountable to deadlines, and deliverables. As a member of one of these groups, understand that your contributions and participation lead to the autonomy that you are looking for. Look to include members of other generations in your groups as they have a knowledge bank that not even Google can provide. They will help keep you on track, and together you can symbiotically move forward. Don't worry if you fail. It will happen. It happens to everyone. Don't get so caught up with the trophy that you forget why you are there. Own your failure, learn from your failure, and grow towards your desired outcome. The tribe will be there for you.

CHAPTER 9

Communicate

"To effectively communicate, we must realize that we are all different in the way that we perceive the world and use this understanding as a guide to our communication with others". – Tony Robbins

One of my leaders came into my office to discuss an issue she was having, and like a good leader, I stopped what I was doing, turned my chair behind my massive desk, and faced her. While she was discussing her concerns, I couldn't help but notice my desk, and how distracting it was. I had a laptop with my e-mail scrolling, a cell phone, an I-Pad, a desktop with the property security cameras playing, and that same security screen was mirrored on my wall across from my desk. As this leader talked, I couldn't help but watch both of our eyes dart around the office as movement occurred on the security cameras, my phone vibrated, or e-mails came churning through. In addition, I was seated on the other side of a very large desk that almost served as a barrier between me and the leader. In that small fifteen-minute conversation, we had experienced more than 25 distractions, and we failed to connect on the issue.

As I took note of the state of affairs, I began to change the way that I handled conversations. I first set a meeting with the leader, and when she arrived, I came around to her side of my desk, and sat down at a small table next to her. I ensured that my wall screen was off, my phone was muted, my e-mail was silent, and that we had a chance to speak without interruption. Once these distractions were eliminated, we had a great conversation, connecting on many issues, and resolved her original challenge. That moment was a revelation for me, because I never realized how detrimental passive communication devices can be to the connection process.

As we all know, there are more ways to communicate now than ever before. Phone calls have given way to texts and e-mails, and new social media sites seem to pop up daily offering a variety of ways for us to "connect". In speaking with many leaders, the sheer volume of communication opportunities has become an impediment to actual communication. Leaders of all generations are struggling to figure out the most productive way to deliver a message, and in the process, are losing ground on building the connections needed to be successful.

I had the privilege of presenting workshops on both Millennial Leadership and Communication to a group of executives who were struggling to move the needle with their teams. I had one executive ask if he would have to start tweeting to get his point across, because, in his words, that was never going to happen. Most people around the table started to chuckle, but you could also sense the uneasiness as they anxiously waited for my response. They were relieved when they heard me say that Twitter was a tool, but that if you weren't comfortable using it, then your communication would come off as fake. The questions then turned to what they could do to make a connection.

I went on to tell them that a connection is simply something that happens when two people, or a group of people, share a commonality that leads to achievement of a goal or task. The base premise being that points of commonality lead to conversations, and conversations lead to connections. The important thing is: that communication should be about the other person, it should be more than just words, it should be simple, and it should be authentic. If you really want to move your team to achieve their goals, then communication should also inspire them. In his book, Everyone Communicates, Few Connect, John Maxwell discusses these topics from his point of view with the intent of providing the reader with tools and guidelines to make those connections. We will explore those topics further through the lens of Millennial Leadership.

Connecting Isn't About You

I recently watched a video of Simon Sinek where he talked about improving your public speaking. One of the main points was that the first thing a speaker should do is determine what they are going to give to the audience. This is an amazing piece of advice that very few people actualize in their daily lives. Most people view each interaction from the paradigm of themselves. What can I get from this interaction, or what will I take away?

As an employer, it is very difficult to constantly look to provide value to your team while trying to be a steward of the bottom line. Each interaction with your team is, either consciously or unconsciously, perceived and assimilated to not only produce a reaction, but also produce a blueprint of how they should or should not act. Most leaders that I have been around choose to interact from the "me" paradigm which, in turn, leads to the same mimicked behavior from the team.

In today's social media society, everyone is used to sending out updates on what they are doing, and keeping cursory contact with hundreds, or thousands, of friends. This trend is shaping how both Millennials and non-Millennials communicate. Listening is a skill, and active listening is an art form. Communication is programmed to go the wrong way if the focus of leaders shifts from their teams to themselves.

While at a conference, I had a chance to speak with a leader that was excited to talk about the ways he was communicating with his team. He told me about his new blog, social templates, e-mail protocol, and daily handout. He was excited about the increased communication, and thought it was a good time to back down on the one-on-ones since the team was getting all of the information they needed now. His systems and processes were very impressive, and his templates were great for what he was trying to do.

As he finished his download, I couldn't help but ask questions about the recipients of his messages. It turned out, that the one thing he forgot in all of his new tools, was the group of people that would be receiving them. He basically carved out a social media program where he would dump information, and then respond via e-mail to cursory questions. He had decided to cancel his one mechanism which ensures that he will build a connection with each team member, and he removed the personal portion of his communication.

This leader forgot that the comments, questions, and feedback that our teams give us is what drives the communication we provide. If we simply send nothing but one-way communication, then we will fail to connect and engage with our teams. Millennials require two-way communication and, while they understand how to digest one way communication, they also become disenchanted when they feel they are not part of the solution or bigger picture. Communication should not be about the leader, it has to be about the employee. No employee cares as much about trendy apps or new formats as they do about being heard and engaged. There is not a product on the market that listens for you, and then uses that information to build a connection with your team.

Leaders should have their teams in mind when they communicate. Even if you are delivering a message, you should constantly be thinking about how it will add value to those that are receiving it. Yes, Millennials have dozens of ways to communicate, but the only one that matters is the one that works. If you are genuine, and have your audience in mind, then you will be received. If your communication lacks authenticity and is simply you talking at your team, then they will not respond.

An authentic style with a mindset on others is not a natural process, thus it will require time and effort to adopt. In many cases, this will simply be a cyclical exercise in practicing and evaluating. However, once you are comfortable with this style, you will notice an immediate change in the way that you perceive your role as an employer, and you will also appreciate how your team receives your direction.

This concept was hard for me to adopt as a leader. I always had a very "hands-on" style of leadership which was perceived to be authentic and for others. In actuality, I was merely looking for a way to be recognized so that I could move up the corporate ranks. This dueling agenda often caused my message to lack substance, requiring the sweat of my brow to make up the difference. As I progressed, and became a leader of more savvy leaders, this style began to fail. I remember sitting with a department head and asking them to go a direction with a project that they weren't comfortable going. They told me that the research pointed to the project being bad for the team, but I knew that if we pulled it off, then I would be promoted again. Naturally, I was not able to sell the time and effort needed to succeed, and the leader lost respect for me during the process. That interaction made me realize the value of authenticity and, as a result, I learned a lot from the failure. I took the blame for the project going poorly, and watched someone else get promoted over me. The unintended side effect was that my leader regained her respect for me. She told me that, by taking the blame, she knew I understood that the decision was bad for the team, and she knew that I would start thinking about them before I thought about my own advancement. It was a tough lesson, but one that reshaped my future as a leader.

Connect Beyond Words

Most people, at this point in their careers, have heard that 93% of communication is non-verbal. That your message is communicated through your body language and tone. The words you use only account for 7% of what is understood. If you did not know that, then understand that how you say things is infinitely more important that what you actually say. So, spend time not only thinking about what you will say, but how you will say it.

In today's society, there are evolving barriers to communication that are keeping people from connecting. The largest barrier to communication in the workplace may actually be the cell phone. I know that cell phones have provided an increased amount of functionality that can deliver almost any piece of information in the world to your fingertips, but at the same time, they have also become almost as effective as mosquito repellent. Use them in public and people stay away from you. Occasionally one gets through, but as a rule, people just don't come near you.

Cell phones have been a growing concern in the Hospitality industry, so I have become accustomed to looking for them everywhere I go. If you go to any restaurant, or walk through any mall, you will see a sizeable percentage of the population with their heads down, soaking up the warm blue light provided by their mobile device. The enormous potential of these devices is torn down by the communication disadvantage that they pose in the connection process.

I have two meetings every week that are fixed on my calendar. The first is my Executive Committee which consists of department heads, and my assistant. The other meeting is with every other leader on property, excluding the Executive Committee. The first meeting is about half Millennials, and the second meeting is about 90% Millennials. The Executive Committee meeting usually features a few leaders checking their phones throughout the meeting. Most of the time, they try to hide it, and other times, they are just blatantly checking their e-mail, texts, etc. They are always so afraid to miss a note or communication, that they often miss what is happening around them. They don't see any problem with it; besides, they see me doing it all the time, so they think it is fine.

My second meeting, surprisingly enough, rarely—if ever— has anyone checking their phones. Occasionally, someone will tell me that they have a family issue and they need to keep up with it, or someone will forget to silence their ringer, but 95% of the time, the phones are put away and they are engaged. It took me months to notice the difference in the two meetings, but when I did, I couldn't help but ask my Millennials in the second meeting why they didn't check their phones all the time. They replied, almost in unison, that it is disrespectful, and they can't focus on the meeting. I was shocked. For a generation that is so connected to their mobile devices, they understand that using a cell phone poses a massive barrier to communication. The non-verbal signals that it sends, tells the individual or group that you are more interested in what is happening on that little box than what is happening with them. They have all grown up with cell phones, so their understanding of their place in business may be more advanced than ours.

After that conversation, I implemented a "no cell phone" policy in my Executive Committee meetings, and for myself in all other meetings. We have a table with a cloth on it at the entrance of the conference room. Everyone puts their phones down, so we don't have an issue with distractions. Imagine if you carry that attitude forward to the common spaces of your work environment. People see you walking down the hallways, not acknowledging anyone, clicking away on your cell phone, and the non-verbal cues that are being perceived are that you have no desire to connect. It becomes virtually impossible to turn it on and off, so instead of picking and choosing when you want to engage, people simply start assuming that you will abandon your conversation with them for the buzzing master in your pocket.

As employers, we need to take a page from our younger counterparts, and set the correct example. Use your cell phone for the powerful tool that it is, but don't let it act as a force field guarding you from any interactions with people while you are in its proximity.

You need to be very deliberate about where, and when, you use your phone. Just think about your personal life. I am sure that you have seen the disconnect with your children that occurs, when you fire up your phone. They are required to love you, or at least tolerate you, because you are their parent. Your employees have no such contract with you, so you can bet that if you choose your phone over them, you will never be able to engage or connect with them.

Connectors Keep It Simple

I love to go to meetings or have conversations with people that simply talk to hear themselves talk. I hope you sensed my sarcasm through the text, and understand that there is nothing worse than someone that will filibuster on any topic, just for the sake of buying time to come up with a real answer. Unfortunately, these people are everywhere. In my experience, I have found that leaders do not like feeling that there is something they do not know. So, instead of simply saying that they don't know, or asking for time to think about it, they will talk in circles until they come up with an actual answer.

Many leaders today forget that people are communicating in 140 characters or less, or are simply using pictures to send their message. As leaders, if we produce long winded memos, over-built presentations, or unfocused conversation, then we will lose the participation of our younger leaders. This generation is encouraging concise communication that is easy to digest, and simple to respond to.

As I have grown in the business world, I have seen communication evolve dramatically, and each time the preferred method gets shorter. When I was in college, we took a whole class designed around shortening our message to get people to listen. The desired outcome of the class was what people have come to refer to as business communication, but now the further evolution of that same communication is a paired down slide show, or text message.

Woodrow Wilson once said, "If I am to speak ten minutes, I need a week for preparation. If an hour, I am ready now." He understood the complicated nature of keeping things simple. One would think that if you were asked to keep things simple, then the process would be easier. The 28th President of the United States knew that if you want to deliver a simple, concise message, it takes planning and development well before you can hope to execute. Too often, we fail to connect because our message is either too long, or too short and ill prepared. As we move to simplify our communication, we should always make sure that the message is well thought out and delivered concisely to ensure engagement and connection.

Connections Must Be Authentic

I frequently speak to executives that feel like the key to all of their issues lies with a better understanding and execution of social media. High-level people are hired to manage the brand image of the company on-line, and whole departments are dedicated to creating a social media presence. They work tirelessly to build a consistent image that is supported by robust articles, carefully researched blogs, and highly monitored Facebook, Twitter, YouTube, and Instagram feeds. I marvel at how quickly all of their efforts can be torn apart by a CEO or Executive that decides they are going to put information out on social media, bypassing the controls, and deliver a message that people know to be fake, in a manner not consistent with the medium.

I had a friend that worked for a large corporation and, one night, while we were out together, he showed me a string of tweets that were coming in on his page. The COO of his company had decided that he was going to use Twitter to convey information to the team, and he just sent out his first tweet. It's not a horrible idea, except that he didn't understand how brief he needed to make his content so his one 140-character tweet evolved into 7 tweets carrying a full chain of consciousness through the message. My friend chuckled, rolled his eyes, and deleted his COO. In one communication, the inauthentic delivery of the COO alienated his Millennial subordinates because he simply tried too hard to be something that he is not.

As I mentioned earlier, it's not always about the medium, but rather the message. Some of the most effective communication I have seen in the workplace were videos that were recorded by leaders and shared with the team. They would record no more than 60 second messages that would play on screens, tablets, or phones throughout the organization. The message was simple, clearly delivered, and in a format that people could easily digest. Team members were able to connect with the non-verbal cues, and any imperfections almost added credibility to the message. The authentic nature of the communication established a connection with the team that left them engaged, and looking for more.

Connections Should Inspire

I attended a wonderful function where the local high school students that participated in the magnet culinary programs prepared all of the food for a fundraising dinner to support their programs. Like most of these events, there was a silent auction, and of course a number of presenters. The last presenter was the head of the school district. He had his PhD, and was a well-respected man in the community. He was charged with closing the event, and leaving all of the sponsors, and donors with a sense of connection that will inspire them to want to maintain their support of the program.

He started his speech off predictably, thanking everyone in attendance. Behind him were the chefs of the evening, and he solicited a round of applause for them. After that, he began about five minutes of talks about himself. After a couple of minutes, about half of the room were already engaged with their cell phones, and that number continued to climb with each passing minute. He seemed to begin to realize that he was losing the crowd and, out of nowhere, he executed a hard stop. As the seconds rolled by, people started to look up from their phones, and within 30 seconds, the whole room was looking back at him. You could tell that he was deviating from his script, and the next 120 seconds became the emphatic message that the board and donors were looking for. He used the remaining two minutes to talk directly to the audience, and to give them a call to action. He admitted that he and his team would not be the ones that teach this next generation of young people to be successful, but that the people in the room would have to take action and become involved in the lives of our developing youth. His two-minute call to action was so passionate and impactful that the crowd went from staring at their phones to providing a standing ovation.

The next day, I found myself e-mailing him and asking what I could do. I offered my services free of charge, and began to work with his team on developing a message that would be impactful to our future leaders. His call to action was an inspiration for me because he realized during that thirty second pause that his message needed to be about the young people standing behind him, and the crowd in front of him. Not himself. He realized that his mission was to add value to the young people in his care, and not to solicit donations. His message included nothing about the next event, or about remaining silent auction items, or even about donations yet to give for the evening. It was simple, elegant, and served others.

The Millennial generation is looking to be connected to a cause, and to make an impact. Leaders need to be authentic, not because people will see through them if they are not, but because authenticity inspires others to action. If your team knows that you are working to better someone other than yourself, then they will follow you, and may even become connected to the things you are passionate about.

When you inspire others, you create a sense of trust and engagement that can only be found through genuine connections. Connectors inspire by not only thinking of others, but also creating calls to action that motivate people to do things they did not think was possible. Sometimes, inspiration can cause a movement or quantum leap, and other times, it simply elicits a first step. That one first step can change the way an organization operates forever.

If you are a Millennial and reading this, be willing to assimilate other communication styles into your daily routine. You may love text messages or videos, but realize that your boss probably doesn't feel comfortable there. If you meet them where they are, they will be much more willing to meet you where you are. Communication methodology is one of those things that you could actually teach your non-millennial co-workers. Don't be afraid to help someone understand the value of brevity, but you must do so, understanding how they have communicated this way all of their lives. When you are given the opportunity to influence how communication is conducted in your organization, remember that it shouldn't necessarily be about you, it should be authentic, and it should be simple. If you can be patient, constructive and informative, you will be able to bring your team closer to where you are instead of forcing them to awkwardly venture there on their own. If you like it when you get a hand written "thank you" card, then tell them, so that the cards don't get replaced with texts, e-mails, or social media posts. The perfect method of communication is most likely a combination of what you like, and what they already do. Communication can be the single great differentiator between loving your job, and looking for a new place to work. Be active in ensuring that you are part of the solution, and not part of the problem.

CHAPTER 10

Teaching is the Future

*"Dig your well before you're thirsty". —
Seth Godin*

One of the primary drivers for Millennials choosing a new job is the opportunity for personal growth and development. This concept seems simple enough, but as employers everywhere start to peel back the layers of the onion, they realize that it is an expansive and complicated issue. Most organizations are not built to service the individual development needs of their teams. Rather the concept of mass customization of the employee experience has just started to permeate organizations. Business are just now starting to realize that there are systems and processes available that can provide customized learning experiences to a great deal of their teams through a standardized package.

A trend that is starting to emerge is training leaders to be teachers. Businesses everywhere are starting to invest in train-the-trainer programs to help push messages out. In addition to that, they are teaching leaders to identify those points of learning to create differentiation within development plans, and produce an employee growth experience around that. Leaders are being taught to harness the individual strengths of their teams, versus trying to mitigate their weaknesses. People at every level are realizing that you can no longer just show someone how to do their jobs, you must find ways to show them how to grow, and develop systems to help them get there. Without these systems, businesses become less attractive to top job-seeking talent.

I worked for a hotel once that had enjoyed a great deal of success before I arrived. They were able to service guests at a world-class level, the facility was immaculate, and there were systems and processes in place to make sure everything was delivered consistently. At first glance, it was an amazing opportunity that I walked into. As I started to study the property more, however, I realized that, while results were great, retention was not. There were very few systems in place to grow talent from within. Additionally, new hires were put through standardized training packages, and nothing was customized from that point. The turnover was well over 100% the first year, and it was very difficult to attract and retain talent.

We decided to train the senior leaders and supervisors to customize development plans and add value individually. This program was rolled out with tools, and programming designed to customize the learning experience for the team while still falling within a system. The program began to really take off when we started offering classes on personal growth. When we stopped focusing on the individual's connection to the job, and started growing them as a person, we found that our engagement numbers and retention improved drastically. We shifted our culture, and began to offer several growth opportunities a month taught by different people on different subjects. As leaders became educators, they became more connected to the team and productivity increased as well.

Teaching cannot just be the responsibility of Human Resources. They are shepherds of programs designed to train people on a large scale. Hardly are they in a position to affect personal growth in the workplace. Many businesses today have opted to introduce robust on-line content that is designed to give their teams access to a multitude of educational opportunities. Unfortunately, that content rarely connects to people, and it definitely does not inspire them.

If Millennials value personal growth and development, then organizations need to train their leaders to become teachers that can create individualized lesson plans designed to kindle growth in their teams. Leaders need to be trained to spot teachable moments, and to use them to build a connection with their new leaders and employees. As they create these personalized experiences, they will automatically increase retention and morale.

I read an article on LinkedIn that provided hiring and retention data on Millennials in the workplace. Most of it was pretty standard, and I didn't really see anything that needed to be commented on. That being said, I did check the comments to see what other people were saying about. As I scrolled through the responses, it was almost exclusively HR recruiters with their opinions about Millennials. One comment in particular was a rant about the fact that Millennials don't stay in one job anymore, so recruiting has become a much bigger problem as positions are constantly opening or in transition.

I could not help but start to formulate a response that simply turned into too much content to be relayed in that medium. Maybe we, as employers, need to start looking at turnover and recruitment in a different light. The linear progression model that we have all used forever is no longer the path that this generation plans on taking. In their book The Corporate Lattice: Achieving High Performance in the Changing World of Work, Cathleen Benko and Molly Anderson describe an employment paradigm where progression is no longer linear, but rather follows a lattice progression. Moves made by individuals can be in a multitude of directions depending on their interest, personal lives, or changing priorities.

If we accept the lattice as the new progression model then recruitment looks completely different. Recruiters could literally be targeting internal recruits for cross-training programs, or cross-functional groups designed to expand the overall knowledge of the team members while giving them the tools they need to move in whatever direction they need to, on the lattice structure. Education within the workplace will be a free-flowing cascade of information that is designed to go in every direction as the recipients will constantly be in a different place in their development. With employees at every level able and willing to move in both directions, the ability to fill positions becomes very easy.

When recruiters have to bring talent in from the outside, then they have a model to attract the best applicants, and teachers in place to ensure that the model continues to work. While this may seem like a lofty structure, the reality is that it is already happening in many of the most successful organizations. An eye on internal recruitment, with the understanding that a promotion for that individual may actually be a traditional demotion, would open up opportunities for not only recruiters, but businesses to have a sufficiency of talent at every level.

Creating leaders that are teachers in the workplace will be a non-negotiable reality of our future. Some people may say that this is nothing new, that leaders have always had to be teachers, and they would be right. The difference is that leaders are now responsible for customizing the experience for each individual, which will naturally result in them having to develop content and execute on learning initiatives. This concept is a vast departure from a work environment that has always heavily relied on Human Resources to produce the education for the team. Teachers will be the future of successful organizations.

If you are a Millennial reading this, understand that you must be an active participant to receive the benefits of this type of education. School did not prepare you for the workplace because there was never a way to connect the tangible benefits of an education to the reality of your life. If you want the flexibility to dictate your level of responsibility, then you need to be prepared to move in many directions, and that requires a solid amount of education. It will also be incumbent on you to actually use the information that you are being given. If you would like it in a different format, or you need more, than you need to step up and say that. Don't be afraid to speak to your employers about what your desired personal and professional growth goals are, and don't miss the chance to act on the opportunities they give you to achieve them. If personal growth and development opportunities are truly important to you, then you need to be ready to put in the work that accompanies those goals, as your employer cannot help you with work ethic.

CHAPTER 11

Practical Application of the Millennial PACT

"Without execution, 'vision' is just another word for hallucination". – Mark V. Hurd

There has been a great deal of information shared to this point, and the overarching theme is that there is a way for employers and employees of multiple generations to engage in a manner that produces growth for all parties involved. In this chapter, we will discuss how an organization can adopt these principles, and what Millennials can do to be successful. As we outline the steps to success, employers need to focus on how they can add value to their Millennial counterparts, and the Millennials need to consider what they can do to play a role in their own personal growth and development.

CARE Model

I have always worked for large corporations, and what I find is that there is always a hefty list of acronyms to accompany every situation. I have already introduced you to the PACT model, and now we are going to look closer at the CARE model. Following this model will help your organization, business, department, or small group improve your work environment, and set you up to create the PACT that we identified earlier.

The CARE model consists of four parts. The first part is to do a current practices assessment. Next, you will ask questions of your operation and team to ensure you are heading in the right direction with your resolution. Then you will be a sterling representative of the change that you are going to make within your organization. Finally, you will evaluate the success of your changes.

Current Practice Assessment

Step 1: Culture Review –

In this step, you are going to want to review every aspect of your culture, and determine how well it has permeated your organization. This is always a tough exercise, because the people at the top always feel like the message is received, and the people at the bottom rarely receive it. I find that you can assess your penetration by going to the line level of your organization and asking them if they know the mission statement of the company. In most cases, they cannot recite it. That isn't necessarily a horrible thing, but it can be, if you ask them to articulate the spirit of the company and they cannot come close to what you are trying to accomplish. When this happens, it is time to find a way to energize your culture.

While you are going through this process, take note of any business units, departments, or even employees that seem to be enlivening the mission statement, or spirit of the company. If you find patches of connection then you can usually look back at the leaders of those areas, and start to formulate processes for spreading your message through their successes. If you cannot find anyone that is having success with your message, then you may need to take a stronger look at the message. The mission of the company has to resonate with the organization in order to create the connection you need to attract and maintain your Millennial workforce.

Step 2: Communication Overview

The next step in working towards building an environment conducive to Millennial success is to evaluate the existing communication methods that you have at your disposal in your organization. How does a message get communicated from various levels? Are e-mails being sent with an understanding that everyone is actually reading them? Is there a newsletter, communique, or other written document that goes out? How do people receive their daily alignment? What social media channels do you already have access to? Are there any third-party vendors involved in the communication process? How many people have cell phones, and actively use them? What is your team's level of access to technology like tablets, laptops, or desktops?

Again, are there any individuals, departments, branches, or other aspects of the organization that seem to be dialed in from a communication standpoint? Just like with culture, these examples will act as future models. Make sure you understand exactly why their communications are successful, and that it is not just a function of the personnel or proximity.

In this step, you will also want to evaluate the communication strengths at each level. Is your CEO a great orator, but poor with e-mail? Are your line level employees already successfully using apps and texts to communicate between each other, and who exactly is in the circle of communication? Are some of your messages reaching parts of the team, and are they well received? Why aren't those same messages reaching other levels of teams? All of these questions will provide a profile of not only the available means of communication, but also the strengths that can act as a base for future growth.

Step 3: Recruiting and Retention Practices

You will want to now evaluate your recruiting and retention practices. To start with recruiting, are you meeting your future team members where they are, or are you simply using what has always worked? Many businesses are content with recruiting like they always have, and only switch methodologies when the well runs dry. What channels are your job postings being publicized through? Where are your recruiters focusing their efforts? How quickly are you reaching out to candidates after they apply? Is there a mechanism to audit stagnant requisitions to prevent your future talent from walking? Is the talent that is being hired in line with the company mission and vision? Are the people interviewing, trained well enough to bring in top talent that matches the profile that your organization is trying to build?

Once you have reviewed how you get candidates, you need to do an honest assessment of how you are retaining them. What does your on-boarding process look and feel like, and is it in line with your mission? What sort of training is the new recruit receiving in their respective area? Are there any weekly, monthly, or quarterly follow-up meetings that occur with new employees? What is your short-term retention rate?

These are extremely important steps because you need to know how talent is entering your organization, and if it is staying. In many cases, businesses find that their methodology has become stagnant on both fronts, and as the workforce is evolving, their processes are not. You will also learn that the easiest time to connect with your employees is within their first six months. They worked hard to be able to join the team, and you worked hard to get them there. The synergies and excitement are at an all-time high, so now is when you should be capitalizing on the momentum. Too many businesses wait too long to create connections with their team, and the longer the employee is with the organization, the harder it is to connect them to the mission or vision.

Step 4: Evaluate Your Training

The final piece of your current state evaluation process is to take a hard look at what you offer for training. Most companies can check off some easy boxes because they have some sort of orientation, leadership training, and on-line university. Don't be discouraged if your organization doesn't have any of these, it just means that there will be some low-hanging fruit to pick up as we look at solutions. In addition to the formal programs that are available at an enterprise level, dig deeper to see what is being done by individual departments, or individual contributors as there may be gold hiding in there. If you have wildly successful programs then highlight them. If you have programs that are lightly utilized, or poorly received, then note those as well.

As you are going through these programs, try and figure out who the actual end user of the training is. Is this training adding value, or meeting a compliance standard? What are the key takeaways, and what is the retention rate on the message? If you were to remove the program, who would it hurt? What holes are left to fill to address the needs of your team? Do any of your programs address the mission of your company, and if so, what weight is being given to that program as compared to others? Are any of the programs attractive to Millennials, and if so, why? These are all great questions that will simply help you collect a baseline. Once you have collected the current status of your organization, it is time to move on to asking questions.

Ask Questions

> *"The quality of a leader cannot be judged by the answers he gives, but by the questions he asks". – Simon Sinek*

Now that you have built a picture of the current state of your operation, business, or organization, it is time to work on changes that can make an impact with your retention, and future recruitment of Millennial talent. The first thing to do is to take a hard look at the programs that you are not actively using or have deemed ineffective through the process, to determine if you need to keep allocating resources there. These programs could be part of your cultural initiatives, a communication methodology, a class or on-line university, or even a recruiting and retention strategy. It is very important to note those programs that you have been allocating resources to, and have been poorly attended or utilized. If you identified it through the process as ineffective or questionable, it needs to go on one list.

The next step is to look at those programs that have a moderate perceived value and bundle those together on a list. These programs will usually require a minimal investment of money or time, and will yield mixed to moderate results. The program value may be overstated by occasional success, or may be masked by successive failures with no growth. Either way, they do not consistently produce the results that you want to achieve, however, they may have potential if modified.

Finally, you want to identify all of the things that are going well for you in any areas that you identified. What messages or communication channels are penetrating the team? What training programs are frequently used or talked about? Are there leaders you discovered that "get it", and do their teams show it in their success? Hold on to the cultural initiatives that have permeated the organizations, and at the same time, make sure you capture any individual effort as well.

Once you have these three lists, then you should start with the list that is working for you. Analyze these programs to see why they are connecting with your target audience, and if the key elements can be reproduced. Is there someone, a business unit, or division that is driving their success? These programs will get you wins, and will help your strategy gain momentum. If you do not have any recruitment or retention successes, communication methods, training initiatives, or cultural programs that produce wins for you, then you need to start looking elsewhere for wins.

This is where asking the right questions will lead to better initiatives and execution. Look at your competition, and see how they have been successful. Most people cannot help but get their successes posted on the internet. Your competitors are no different. If they have something that is working for them, which you don't appear to have, then try and analyze the successful elements and see if you can infuse those into a new or existing program to gain leverage off the successes that someone else has proven. One-on-ones with your top team members at every level will also produce a bevy of great ideas, and future wins. In these meetings, you are going to want to lead with the reasons that the team members are sitting with you. Highlighting their accomplishments will get them excited to participate, and will instill the confidence that you need to move the needle.

In addition to benchmarking, you can start to analyze the other two tiers of your lists. In the moderate tier, begin to ask why the highs are high, and the lows are low. Look to what is causing the inconsistency, and determine if there is a variable that you can modify. If the programs simply are bad programs then get rid of them. Learn from your failures, and move on. If you can salvage success and turn a program into a win, then it is worth the effort.

Asking good questions of not only your processes and methodology, but also your team and competitors will lead to insight that will produce results. Through this process, you will have a number of programs, communication methods, and teachable materials to jumpstart your retention and recruitment. Start with the cultural programs that enhance your mission and connect your team to the "why" of your organization. Once those are in process, then begin to work on the strongest programs on your list. As your team increases their engagement, they will be more willing to go out on a limb for a new initiative that you roll out. Your successes will be well publicized in our viral society, leading talented people to want to work for you, and the talent you have to want to stay with you.

Represent Change

> *"Be the change you wish to see in the world"* – Mahatma Gandhi

Making changes in the way that you do business is key to the future success of your organization. Each change that engages the team will produce results for whatever your goal may be. As a leader, regardless of your generation, you will be responsible for being the blueprint for what others should and should not be. Frequently, programs are launched, and executives don't understand why they don't work. What I find is that, most of the time, the initiative comes from the top down, but the example goes from the bottom up.

One of the key pillars to success with Millennial integration is the prevalence of authenticity in your organization. A leader that does not act in accordance with the vision they have laid out is simply casting the first stone in the bucket that will eventually sink the ship. Lack of authenticity is a deal breaker for the new leaders and employees entering your organization. If cultural jargon is just that— jargon— then connections won't be made, and employees will start to look elsewhere. The vicious cycle of constantly having to recruit and retain will be furthered by the self-inflicted turnover that occurs because the organization is not aligned from the top down.

Even leaders that show vulnerability through the change initiatives are much more strongly received than those that simply quit when things become uncomfortable. I worked for a leader once that used to make us recite the company mission statement nearly daily. He would frequently ask us what it means, and how we can apply it. At the time, I didn't see value in the exercise, but now I can see how it would be beneficial for the younger leaders. The only issue was that we would talk about how to treat guests, and how to treat each other, and our leader would simply tear people down in public as part of his management style. We had a great deal of turnover, and the ones that stayed were miserable. Eventually, when he left, the guest satisfaction scores began to rise again as the team began to build a relationship with the new leader. This is a great example of a leader that didn't walk the talk, and it ended up costing him his job and a solid piece of his team.

Evaluate Your Success

The final step in the CARE model is to evaluate your success. I mentioned a cultural initiative earlier that I implemented at one hotel. This initiative revolved around the book The Energy Bus, by John Gordon. We had a great deal of success rallying the team around a message that was simple enough for everyone to understand and communicate. Our engagement results, financial results, and guest satisfaction results were through the roof that year. The leadership team continued to ride that message into the following year, but as time wore, on the message wore off. We weren't taking the time to evaluate what was working with an eye to keeping it fresh.

There are going to be staple programs that are timeless, and will always be with your team. These programs will provide a sense of security to new employees as they enter your organization, and will sustain a connection between the employees that stay year after year. Unfortunately, the vast majority of new initiatives come with a shelf life. Once a new program reaches a certain penetration level, it will need to be refreshed or replaced. One of the great shortcomings of many leaders I have worked with, is that they celebrate the same success over and over again. They fail to realize that success has a shelf life, and that it requires constant evaluation.

In my experience, a program that has been unchanged in a year is most likely reaching its critical penetration. At that point, leaders need to start the CARE Model all over again with an understanding that what works today won't necessarily work tomorrow. This process is great for younger leaders as it will always make sure that their opinions are heard, and that they have input in the future of the organization. The core programs will always remain, but the initiatives that engage the Millennial generation will have to be kept fresh to keep pace with the rapidly evolving society, retention, and learning cycles.

If you are a Millennial employee or leader reading this, then the CARE Model is not just for your employers, it is also for you. Take this model and apply it to your environment from the bottom up. Do a cultural inventory of your organization from your point of view. Ask the questions that will help to create the change you want to see. Look hard at your habits and practices to make sure you are representing the organization that you want to see built around you. Finally, constantly evaluate your paradigm to make sure that you don't need to make adjustments to meet the changing climate. By doing this, you will ensure that you know what you want so that when your leadership structure looks to involve you, ideas are already generated and you are ready to participate. If you simply want things to change, but bring nothing to the table, then you will be marginalized, not because of your generation, but because you weren't prepared. If employers will go to this length to engage you, then make sure you are supporting their attempts.

      Please feel free to reach out to me to ask questions, start a dialogue, or even tell me I'm crazy. My website is www.jlhleadership.com/. Thank You!

Conclusion

I hope that you have found value in this book. I have been on both sides of the generational question most of my career, and truly feel that the answer to the "Millennial Question" really lies in our ability to connect our commonalities and explore the new teaching paradigm. I am well aware that you have probably read some of this information before, and that the leadership principles contained in this book are not groundbreaking. I have read hundreds of books and articles on leadership, and most of them boil down to the same advice. What that means is that everyone has had access to the same teachings and information for a very long time.

The major difference in all of these books is that someone presents the information in a way that resonates with you, and it inspires you to action. Dale Carnegie, John Maxwell, Stephen Covey, Simon Sinek, they all are giving you the same principles. My goal with this book was to provide you with another point of view to hopefully connect you to the information, and inspire you to action. It may sound insanely simple, but you have to do something to get things done. If this book gave you a call to action to take the first step, then it will have been successful.

This new generation is extremely educated, motivated, and innovative. The progressive leader will see past the stereotypes that have been laid out there that generalize the behavior of a fraction of the generation, and will activate their actual potential. Shifts will have to be made in the way that organizations are run to ensure that their teams are making the connection to their mission. Once employees know why they are working where they are, and why their organization exists, then the buy-in will open the door for future success. Engaged employees, especially Millennials, will attract future employees, and will help to guide you in the best ways to retain them. Creative promotional structures, training and personal growth opportunities, personalized employment experiences, and the support of groups will help to ensure that your organization is an employer of choice and a place to stay in the future.

About the Author

For more than 20 years I have been a leader or Executive in the hospitality industry, learning from industry giants like Marriott, Hard Rock Hotels and Casinos, and Ritz-Carlton. Being inspired by the spirit to serve took me well past learning world class service for guests, it showed me that world class service has to extend to your team. I understand what it takes to reach unique personalities and inspire them to greatness. I believe that you do not become a leader until you learn to add value to others.

As a speaker, trainer, and Executive Coach I have had the privilege of enhancing the transition experience into the workplace of many new and future leaders. Continuing to lead has provided me with a unique platform to experience what I write about, and continue to add value to others through my efforts.

I am also a husband, and a father to two wonderful children. When I am not serving my family, you will probably find me running. As an avid runner, triathlete, and ultra marathoner I have had the pleasure of experiencing some amazing things like completing an Ironman Triathlon, and running the Grand Canyon. I try not to waste one minute of my life, and hopefully I can help create an environment where you don't feel you are wasting a minute of yours either.

Learn more about CHRIS CANO at JLHLEADERSHIP.com

Notes

Chapter 1

"The children now love luxury....exercise."
http://www.bartleby.com/73/195.html
Simon Sinek, Millennials in the Workplace; (Inside Quest, October 2016):
https://www.youtube.com/watch?v=hER0Qp6QJNU
Seth Godin, International Maxwell Conference, (March 20, 2017)

Chapter 2

"Few will have......generation";
https://www.brainyquote.com/quotes/quotes/r/robertkenn135396.html
Holmes, Ryan, (Oct, 2016) "Move over Millennials: 5 Things you need to know about generation C,
https://www.inc.com/ryan-holmes/move-over-millennials-5-things-you-need-to-know-about-generation-c.html
Jon Gordon, (2007) The Energy Bus, John Wiley & Sons Inc., Hoboken, New Jersey

Chapter 3

"From my very first.....better"
http://www.businessinsider.com/interview-with-virgin-founder-richard-branson-2016-8
Jon Gordon, (2007) The Energy Bus, John Wiley & Sons Inc., Hoboken, New Jersey

PWC Millennials Survey;
https://www.pwc.com/gx/en/issues/talent/future-of-work/download.html
PEW Research Center, Millennials;
http://www.pewresearch.org/topics/millennials/

Chapter 4

"Service to other is…..Earth";
http://www.ibtimes.com/muhammad-alis-life-quotes-20-quotes-honoring-legend-2547134
"a race is a…..understanding";
http://thinkexist.com/quotation/a_race_is_a_work_of_art_that_people_can_look_at/333756.html

Chapter 5

"Management is doing things…..thing";
https://www.entrepreneur.com/article/237484
John Maxwell, (1998) 21 Irrefutable Laws of Leadership, Thomas Nelson Inc., Nashville, Tennessee.

Chapter 6

"You must take personal…..charge of";
http://www.values.com/inspirational-quotes/7267-you-must-take-personal-responsibility-you

Chapter 7

"Conformity is the jailer…..growth";
http://www.beliefnet.com/quotes/inspiration/j/john-f-kennedy/conformity-is-the-jailer-of-freedom-and-the-enemy.aspx

Chapter 8

"Synergy is what happens…..challenge";
http://www.businesswire.com/news/home/20111020005530/en/Stephen-Covey-Releases-Book-3rd-Alternative-Solving

Chapter 9

"To effectively communicate…..others";
https://en.wikiquote.org/wiki/Anthony_Robbins
John Maxwell; (2010) Everyone Communicates Few Connect, Thomas Nelson Inc., Nashville, Tennessee.
"If I am to speak…..now";
http://www.bartleby.com/73/1288.html

Chapter 10

"Dig your well before you're thirsty";
https://www.brainyquote.com/quotes/quotes/s/sethgodin442073.html
Cathleen Benko, Molly Anderson, (2010) The Corporate Lattice: Achieving high performance in the changing world of work, Deloitte Development LLC, Unites States of America.

Chapter 11

"Without execution…..hallucination";
https://www.brainyquote.com/quotes/authors/m/mark_v_hurd.html
Simon Sinek; (2009) Start With Why: How great leaders inspire everyone to action, Penguin Publishing, New York, New York.

"Be the change…..world"; https://www.goodreads.com/quotes/24499-be-the-change-that-you-wish-to-see-in-the

73739105R10074

Made in the USA
Columbia, SC
17 July 2017